BENDING THE TWIG

A memoir

By

Kenneth Goetz

28 May 2002

To Jerry Bolin,
with my best wishes —

Ken Goetz

ISBN: 0 7596 6133 2

This book is printed on acid free paper.

1stBooks - rev. 12/11/01

When you have nothing, you remember everything

-Frank McCourt

Just as the twig is bent the tree's inclined

-Alexander Pope

For Emma and George, who struggled through
shortened lives and set us on our way

For Carol, Betty, and Gary,
who were there

And for Shirley, Gregory, and Anne,
who care

CHAPTER 1

"You're a lucky boy."

Right. Real lucky. And rich. And ten-and-a-half feet tall. I glanced at my grandfather. His eyes, inscrutable behind wire-framed bifocals, focused on the wing joint where his knife worked.

I ripped open the tender skin of my pheasant and stripped off its iridescent plumage, mulling the odd comment. With the point of my hunting knife I dislodged a few pellets from the breast. We sat on low stools in the backyard, cleaning birds after our Saturday afternoon hunt.

"Yep, you're lucky," Grandpa repeated brightly. He was seventy-one, rheumatic but reasonably spry, still working for a living, still accurate with a shotgun. Until that moment I had considered him to be level-headed.

I was sixteen. My younger brother and I lived with our maternal grandparents. Our two sisters were seventy miles away, living with an aunt and uncle. Things were going fairly well for

1

me just then, but calling me lucky was like calling the two dollars in my pocket a fortune.

"This one's hardly shot up at all," I said, slitting open its belly and catching a whiff of guts and blood. I slipped my fingers under the ribs and ripped out the heart and fragments of lung, then the windpipe and gullet. Had someone at that moment predicted that one day I would carve the corresponding organs from a cadaver's chest and call the vital tubes by their more scientific-sounding names, trachea and esophagus, I would have fallen down laughing.

But I would eventually make my way to medical school and troop along with my new classmates into the anatomy laboratory for that first time, our nostrils alert to the unfamiliar air laced with formaldehyde, alcohol, and preserved human flesh, our anxieties concealed beneath shells of exaggerated confidence. Standing before my cadaver, an elderly male gray as slate, I would take up my scalpel - and balk. Though I was adept with my well-honed hunting knife, quick to cut and quick to finish, I hesitated before that preserved gray body, for I had been bruised by Death's power, and that lifeless form recalled loved ones I had lost. But life goes on. I forced myself to press my keen blade into that cold throat - and broke the spell. In the months that followed I calmly sliced through my cadaver's remains with scalpel and scissors, sawed through his bones, cut out his silent heart and gritty liver, probed his rubbery brain, my knowledge expanding as he diminished. But even though I'd learned much since that distant afternoon when my grandfather had called me lucky, I hadn't yet grasped his meaning.

We drew poor cards during the Dakota Thirties and Forties, my family and I. At times we were dead broke, not a dime in the cupboard, not a slice of bread. The weak economy contributed to our misery, but less directly than did cheap whiskey. During our brief flurry at full strength, our family consisted of six: our father, George; our mother, Emma; and four children; Kenneth, Carol, Betty, and Gary.

In the spring of 1928, my father, George Goetz, quick-minded and analytical though his father had permitted him only eight years of schooling, married my gentle mother, Emma Schafer, who had graduated from high school a year before their marriage. She was twenty, he twenty-five. Theirs was a double wedding, the other couple being Emma's brother, Gerhart, and George's sister, Rose. Two families united twice for a single price.

The marriage partners shared similar backgrounds. Both families, the Goetzs and the Schafers, were of the heterogeneous stock often lumped under the rubric, Germans from Russia. And both families had followed similar paths. In 1816, my great-great-great grandfather, Johann Jakob Götz, a wine farmer from the village of Ellhofen, located in what later would become the state of Baden Württemberg, Germany, packed up his wife and children and led a band of followers to the plains of southern Russia where they settled in Glückstal (Lucky Valley), one of nearly two hundred villages populated largely by German immigrants. One year earlier, Conrad Schäfer, the patriarch of my mother's family, had emigrated from the same German area (from the village of Zuffenhausen, now a suburb of Stuttgart and perhaps best known for the glistening Mercedes Benzes that roll off its assembly lines). Conrad settled his family in Borodino, Besserabia. Borodino and Glückstal were located northwest of the Black Sea, within the borders of present-day Moldova.

The Götzs and Schäfers were among thousands of Germans drawn like bees to blossoms to the plains above the Black Sea by the Czar's promises of cash loans, productive land, religious freedom, and exemption from military service. While there, my

3

transplanted German forebears prospered and propagated for the better part of a century, farming from tiny central villages, retaining their native language. When Russia's political conditions deteriorated, a new generation of German-Russians with wanderlust followed their itchy feet to the United States. Upon arrival, my branch of the Schäfers skimmed the umlaut off the a; the Götzs followed the more standard practice of inserting an e after the vowel when removing its umlaut.

One of the grooms in the double wedding, my father George, was among the immigrants; he was born in Glückstal in 1902, and came to this country with his family in 1905. The other groom, and both brides, were first generation Americans.

The Goetzs and Schafers seemed well-matched. Both were farming families who tilled the Dakota soil from dawn to dark with Germanic intensity, doggedly keeping their tools and implements clean, sharp, and oiled. Both families paused each Sunday to worship in the Lutheran church and bellow lusty hymns in German.

Despite their kindred backgrounds, George and Emma were not a perfect match. Troublesome omens hovered over their marriage. George was known to have a taste for bootleg whiskey and beer. He had clashed with his father and had been forced to leave the family home when he was seventeen, though the circumstances, I later learned, favored my father. He was ousted after impulsively grabbing his hot-tempered father from behind one day and preventing him from striking his mother. The older man, his wrath transferred, banished George and booted him from the house with nothing but the clothes he wore.

Emma, a quiet farm girl, was shy and unassertive. She had suffered a violent case of scarlet fever as a child, a disorder that had sown the seeds of her destruction.

Emma and her brother, Gerhart, about 1911

I have a snapshot of the newlyweds taken on the wedding day, the gowned brides holding their bouquets, wind ruffling their hair, the men in suits and bow ties, four pleasant smiles. The grooms stand on the outside, partly behind their brides, with shoulders overlapping. Oddly, George's right shoulder is chopped off, missing. A close inspection reveals a faint line that extends

5

upward and downward from where his shoulder ends, indicating that this photo is a copy of an original that had been snipped and pasted back together to bring George closer to Emma. In the wind on his wedding day he had stood apart.

Gerhart, Rose, Emma, and George on their wedding day in 1928

They wed in Java, a tiny community that sprouted on a windy Dakota plain a century ago. Java lies midway between the east and west coasts of the United States, and equidistant between the equator and the North Pole: latitude 45' 30" N. The latter distinction is shared, give or take a couple of minutes, by Portland, Oregon, and Montreal, Canada - and by Lyon, Milan, and a slice of northern Japan.

Like most Dakota landscapes, the one surrounding Java is stark: an oceanic expanse of grass and grain interrupted by widely scattered clumps of trees and isolated farms. Richly populated with pheasant and prairie song birds, with gopher, hawk, snake, coyote, and skunk, the land is home to relatively few humans. The growing season is short, the farm land marginal, the climate extreme in summer and winter, a good place, as a Dakota expatriate once told me, to be *from*. Although I understand that sentiment now, I would have bristled had I heard it when I lived there. Beauty, in the eye of the beholder, was everywhere then, in artistic mixes of multicolored grains and grasses waving in the wind, in the yellow dots of spindly wild sunflowers, in the sculpted white glare of winter, and, above all, in the boundless land — the infinite space for living.

Our family moved often. At age thirteen I could recall ten different houses we had called home. I disliked the way we bounded from place to place, leaving friends behind, starting over with strangers, doing it again and again. Though I didn't consider it so then, our movement was limited, all within the borders of South Dakota.

Faster than our family grew, it shrank. One heart was stilled with agonizing slowness, another most abruptly. And so we were six, then five, than only four: my two sisters, my brother, and I. I'd like to think that we four youngsters were, like children of Lake Wobegon, above average. The years passed, we grew up, scattered across the country, matured, opened bank accounts. We became, I believe, reasonably good citizens. Each of us produced children of our own, a new generation launched into a realm astonishingly unlike the one that molded us.

When I made my inauspicious arrival as the first-born son of George and Emma, the *Java Herald* dutifully announced it, as it did all community births. From its January 7, 1932, edition: *Born to Mr. and Mrs. George Goetz this afternoon, a fine baby boy. The Herald*

7

congratulates. The newspaper reported that a thick fog had shrouded Java for weeks, that soft snow had fallen on the day preceding my birth, that trees and wires sagged under ice and frost. I was born, appropriately enough, under thick, cold clouds. Though it meant nothing to me then, I later was amused to learn that the heavy cloud of prohibition still drifted over the land when I arrived, that not until a month before my second birthday did the Twenty-first Amendment repeal the Eighteenth and set off the wet and joyous celebration that my father surely joined into with gusto.

Herbert Hoover dawdled in the Oval Office, presiding over the birth of the Great Depression, passively awaiting the prosperity that lurked "just around the corner." His patience unrewarded, his country foundering, he managed to hold on only until I learned to walk with confidence, the very month when Franklin Roosevelt and his New Deal swept Hoover from the White House.

In my earliest memory, the summer when I was two-and-a-half, my mother talks with a peddler inside our front door. I sit near the bottom of the stairway leading to the second floor of our rented home, watching her take a frying pan from the peddler and examine it. Her slender figure stands in profile, her light-brown hair, cut short, curves in to nestle softly at the angle of her jaw. The peddler remains a respectful distance from her. Mother hefts the frying pan by its handle, turns it over to inspect the back, thoroughly enjoying her part of the transaction. No voices, no clashes of the peddler's pans, adorn the scene. I cannot remember the sound of my mother's voice. In the end she bought the pan, seeming quite pleased with herself, and pleasing me by being pleased. This wisp of memory intrigues me not only because it is the most distant one I can retrieve, but also because of what I had forgotten about that time. My mother and I lived alone. My father was away.

It was the mid-thirties. We lived in a two-story frame house on Java's Main Street, at the southern edge of the densely-packed commercial district jammed with saloons, hotels, grocery stores, lumber yards, a post office, drug store, photographic shop, newspaper office, and more. Our family's wandering had already begun. The house on Main Street was the fourth dwelling we had occupied since my birth.

About seven hundred people populated Java then, the vast majority of German origin, many still speaking their native dialect at home and in the streets. My parents had learned German before English, but they rarely spoke it in our house, and never to me, I suspect because they viewed their German as the language of immigrants and saw no reason for their offspring to learn it. Throughout my childhood I was as innocent of German as I was of Boolean algebra.

My early days in Java were carefree. For amusement I often pedaled my small tricycle along the sidewalk from our end of the block to the other end, grinning at everyone I passed. On those rare times when a coin tingled electric in my pocket, I headed directly for the upper end of our block and parked my trike outside Lange's Mercantile Store, where I exchanged my penny for a box of Snaps, little licorice-flavored pieces. Patrolling the sidewalk on my tricycle with the taste of Snaps lingering on my tongue was absolute bliss. An outgoing cub, I eagerly sought companionship with anyone who wandered by. Though the streets of Java weren't filled with throngs of pedestrians, there was no shortage of passers-by willing to exchange a word or two with a cheerful innocent.

My next favorite place was my grandparents' farm. Mother's parents, Jacob and Katherine Schafer lived three miles east of

Java. I was deposited there from time to time to sample farm life. A single scene stands out. I toddle around the farm yard, tagging after my grandfather. A white calf wriggles through a fence and trots toward the road. Grandpa Schafer goes to round it up, I happily helping. Taking my duties seriously, I pick up a small stick and run toward the calf. I shout. "Get going, you thon of a bitsth."

Whether I was truly tongue-tied at that age, or whether my Aunt Ella, who lived with her parents on the farm and loves to tell the story, adopts that pronunciation for effect, I cannot say. Grandpa Schafer, sturdy stick in his own hand, storms over to scold me for my salty words, surprising me. Why did my saying the words make them bad? Grandpa indignantly reports my unseemly remark to Grandma, who is busily picking beans from her garden. As the accusation flies from his mouth, he recognizes too late his tactical error, and notes how easily the familiar phrase slips from his tongue.

"And where," Grandma says, straightening up and glaring at my grandfather, "did he learn such language?"

The economy was on its knees, shattered. This situation explains, at least partly, why my father is absent from my earliest memories. Unable to find work in Java, he had in desperation joined the horde of individuals nationwide who took to the road to find employment. Before leaving town, he had managed to snare only the occasional job, taking seasonal work with farmers: breaking earth with a horse-drawn plow for one, seeding with a drill and team of horses for another, shocking grain for a third. He and his younger brother, Fred, had operated a town dray line for a while, two strong former farm boys willing to haul with a team and a wagon whatever needed hauling. Their venture failed. Horses and wagons were common in Java then, and few townsmen had money to hire work done. One of Dad's sisters, Aunt Rose, remembers one of their more successful days.

"Your mother was so excited. She said, 'George brought home some money, so we'll be able to...' — I can't remember what she wanted to do, but that's not the important part. What I remember vividly is your mother's beaming smile, her pure happiness when suddenly having a dollar or two to spend."

In my dewy-eyed innocence, our early period of family indigence passed over me as unnoticed as a blanket drawn gently over a sleeping child. I ate my fill, saw no evil, met no violence, knew nothing of war, heard not a word of the notorious criminals who came to bloody ends in 1934, though it was a vintage year for slaughtering thugs. A short list: Bonnie and Clyde gunned down near Shreveport, John Dillinger riddled outside a Chicago theater, "Pretty Boy" Floyd dispatched with machine guns in Ohio, and "Baby Face" Nelson, pierced by seventeen federal bullets, found limp and bloody in an Illinois ditch. Al Capone had better luck, being thrown into Alcatraz, alive. But in my young world crime was absent. No one carried a gun. People were good.

I had forgotten where my father had gone while he was away, but a yellowed copy of the *Java Herald* brought it back to me. The *Herald's* September 20, 1934, edition carried this item: *George Goetz returned last Friday evening from Glasgow, Montana, where he has been employed on the Fort Peck dam project for the past few months.*

The words flashed through haze and illuminated a scrap of long-shrouded memory. "Daddy!" I run to him as he walks in the front door. He catches my wrists and lifts me up to eye level. I squeal with happiness. He puts me down, pulls me back up. "George, be careful!" Mother cautions.

Another brief item from the same edition of the *Herald* expands the story: Mr. and Mrs. George Goetz took their little son, Kenneth, to Mobridge Saturday to consult Dr. Spiry

11

regarding an injury the youngster had suffered to his wrist while playing.

After Dad returned from Montana, he scoured the town to find work and again found none. But thanks to his sister-in-law, he heard of a job opening not too far away. Aunt Ella, a high school student at the time, learned through her sociology teacher that his father-in-law from Gettysburg was searching for someone to run his sheep ranch.

Word was passed. The man, a Mr. Nelson Gidley, came to Java to talk with my parents. They reached an agreement. Our immediate future suddenly sealed with a quick handshake, we prepared to leave Java for the sheep ranch, site unseen, in late October of 1934. Our departure sparked discussion in Aunt Ella's sociology class.

"We were talking about how hard the times were," Aunt Ella told me. "Our teacher mentioned that a young Java couple had taken a job on a sheep ranch near Gettysburg, and commended them for doing it. He explained that they had chosen to leave family and friends to avoid going on relief. He didn't mention names, didn't have to in a small town like Java. Everyone knew he was talking about George and Emma. In those days we thought a move of fifty miles was a big jump."

Not yet three at the time, and eager to follow my parents anywhere, I made the big jump from town to ranch without a whimper.

CHAPTER 2

The Gidley sheep ranch loomed ahead of us, a lonely cluster of buildings spotted on a range of open grassland stretching to the Dakota sky. When we pulled up to the weathered ranch house, a tight gathering of sheep studied us from their pen west of the house. A larger flock foraged unconcerned on the prairie to the south, grazing on thin grass faded to autumnal brown. The house was one of four structures on the ranch, the others being a long three-walled shed in the sheep pen, its open side facing the house, a large sturdy barn, and an old shack occupied by a grizzled sheep herder. Old Albert, as we came to call the man, was kindly but distant, a man who favored being by himself. He stayed for a few months, showing Dad the ropes, easing him into ranch work, and then moved on to other solitudes.

The ranch lay eight and a half miles south of Gettysburg, a town slightly larger than Java and situated nearer to the center of South Dakota. Though it was an alien world to me, incalculably far from the town we had left behind, a single pencil dot on a basketball-sized globe would easily cover the distance we had moved. I was too young to gauge my parents initial impressions of our new home. Did they look upon the ranch as an opportunity? Or did their relief in having a job dwindle when they saw how remote the place was, how lonely that open land?

The frame ranch house was small, having a kitchen, parlor, and two bedrooms. The floors were soft wood, probably pine. The graying exterior needed paint. As in Java, our toilet was an outdoor privy, this one with a weathered exterior perfectly matching that of the ranch house. Dad's younger brother, Fred, helped with our move and stayed on through mid-winter, working the ranch with Dad. He too had been unable to find work elsewhere and gratefully worked for no pay, only his room and board.

We settled in, my parents and I sharing one of the bedrooms, Uncle Fred taking the smaller one. My large crib, wedged into the southwest corner of our bedroom, plunged me into recurrent nightmares. In those disturbing dreams I crawled anxiously down from my bed and peered under my parents' bed, which was centered along the north wall. Lurking beneath that bed were ferocious lions and tigers growling and clawing, coiled and ready to lunge and chew me to pieces. Those savage beasts set me quivering with terror, yet I could not avoid drifting sleepily into that fantasy. Night after night I scrambled over the rail of my crib and dropped apprehensively to the floor. The frightful beasts never failed to appear, their fangs bared. When my subconsciousness grew weary of that game, I took to falling out of clouds suspended high above the ranch, a vantage point that provided a fine view of the top of our house and barn - and the wooly backs of our sheep - my stomach tickling as I slowly fell toward them, bracing myself for the landing that never came. On other nights I warded off rattlesnakes that skittered noisily down the fender of our pickup truck when I kicked its tires. And each morning, having survived my dangers, I awoke relieved.

Years later, after a friend had read my description of the locations of my crib and my parents' bed in that ranch house bedroom, she told me that my recollection of the layout "troubled" her, an indirect way of saying she didn't believe I could have properly oriented myself in space when so young. In fact, I did. My early ability to square myself with the earth strikes me as quite ordinary, scarcely more advanced than differentiating up from down. Even earlier, while we lived in Java, I knew Main Street ran north-south, that our front door opened to it on the east. South Dakota's orderly layout surely aided my early orientation. Practically all roads in the state - town and country - ran in one of two directions, east-west or north-south.

When we transferred to the open range of the ranch, we found ourselves in the midst of a checkerboard of country roads that ran straight and true around sections of land at one-mile intervals. As ranchers and farmers routinely do, we oriented ourselves by the cardinal directions, spoke of the north road, the south pasture, the clouds to the west. Our compass, though rarely needed, was the arc of the sun. Or the stars. My father introduced me to the Big Dipper on the ranch. He didn't have to tell me it occupied the northern sky.

The sheep ranch was half sky. The rare tree or a low building might obscure a patch of that enormous space, but from practically everywhere I could see the entire heavens. In the spring my father and I watched flocks of sandhill cranes migrate northward. I followed their seemingly slow flight intently, squinting when I first heard their faint musical calls, spotting the distant, thread-like flocks at the end of Dad's finger, watching the threads enlarge and split into individual cranes speeding along on graceful wings, floating their chorus of melodic bells overhead.

Then they grew smaller, became thin threads again, and disappeared in the north. Dad said they were moving, just as we had. I envied the ease with which they traveled. The sky held other wonders.

"Do you see those?" Dad asked me late one spring afternoon, pointing to the west with the cigarette he had rolled by hand. He wore his standard ranch uniform: bib overalls, a cotton shirt with two large breast pockets, work shoes, a porkpie cap. I don't know how tall he was, maybe five-ten. Dad rarely showed emotion, other than an occasional outburst of anger punctuated by a few *God damns* and *Jesus Christs*. Though he wasn't one to hug me, he was unfailingly kind on the ranch. His cool reserve, I suspect, had been ingrained in his own youth. His father, an authoritative figure from the Old Country, had raised his nine children with harsh discipline. Dad improved on that. He didn't gush over me, but he wasn't a strict disciplinarian. He was more of an indulgent master, I the admiring apprentice.

"The clouds?" I said. "Sure." We stood near the sheep pen. A soft breeze carried its distinctive scent our way.

The lower third of the western sky was thick with clouds, their tops a brilliant white, their bellies dark and ominous. I knew the clouds carried a storm. I didn't like storms, didn't like rain or hail pelting our ranch house in darkness, didn't like terrifying lightning, or thunder that rattled our house and bumped over the prairie. The dark clouds worried me.

"Do you see what's on the bottom?"

The smooth lower edge of cloud was interrupted by gray swirls that seemed to come out to peek around. Some poked out far enough to resemble teats on a cow's udder. Three or four swirls stretched down, climbed back up. One appeared to reach the distant ground.

"What is it?"

"Those are tornadoes."

I knew the word. Knew tornadoes were bad and destroyed houses, knew they could kill, but the cloud's teats looked harmless. One might milk them for rain.

"I'll tell Mommy," I said.

I brought her out by the hand. We three, dwarfed by the vast land, observed the plodding storm. I stood small between lean and angular George and slim Emma, listening as they speculated whether the storm was headed our way. Mother wore a dress as she always did, never slacks or jeans, not even on the ranch. She had a tendency to speak softly, to smile shyly. We watched the dark clouds flicker dimly, as if someone had struck a gigantic match inside. Faint, low-pitched grumbles came our way. The darkest part of the cloud bank slowly drifted to the north. We held our position until we were convinced the tornadoes would pass us by.

On the ranch I learned to recite my ABCs. Mother taught me the alphabet, to count, to recite the child's prayer when I went to bed at night. She sat on a straight wooden chair in the kitchen, teaching. I stood dutifully beside her, learning. I didn't yet reach her shoulder when she was seated. In our first lessons, when I recited by rote, the alphabet seemed made of strange big words without meaning: ABCDEFG, and HIJKLMN. After I learned the sequence, she wrote the individual letters on a tablet she held on her lap, linking shape with sound. Taking the tablet, I copied them as best I could, uttering the sound of each.

Then, after weeks of drills, Mother surprised me. She took three letters out of order and wrote them down.

"What does the first one say?" she asked.

"Mmmmm"

"And the last one?"

"Mmmmm." I jumped to the middle letter, made a wild guess. "Mom!"

"That's good Kenny. You learn quickly."

I basked in her praise during those early tranquil lessons, mother instructing child, sharing in her pleasure. What I remember most clearly from those times is my fascination with her light-brown hair, which shimmered in the morning light flooding through the north window, her light-brown hair - and her loving diligence.

When we next visited Mother's parents, I showed off shamelessly for Grandma Schafer, reciting the alphabet, counting to one hundred, identifying simple words I recognized in a magazine. Grandpa and Grandma Schafer had recently moved to another farm as sharecroppers. They never accumulated capital enough to purchase a farm of their own. This new place glittered with attractions. Nestled on the northern edge of Spring Lake, some three miles south of Java, the farmhouse was a rural marvel, one of a kind in that area of Dakota during the Great Depression, and an unlikely rural site for a youngster to be introduced to modern household conveniences. When I stepped into that kitchen for the first time, I instantly saw its magic.

Unlike most Dakota farm houses of that era, this one had electric lights, energized by batteries kept full by a windcharger, or in the rare times when the Dakota winds calmed, by a backup gasoline engine. It amazed me to walk into any room at night and, with the press of a wall switch, throw the entire room into brilliance, a squint-inducing flood when compared to the pitiful glow of our kerosine lamps at the ranch.

And the telephone. The one in Grandma's kitchen was the first I encountered. Its wooden-box frame hung on the north wall, its black mouthpiece centered in front, its black earpiece and cord suspended by a hook on the left side. On the right was the chrome-plated crank used to call the central operator in Java for a connection. Grandma explained how it worked and boosted me up so I could speak into the mouthpiece while Aunt Ella was on the line, speaking from a telephone in Java. I held the heavy receiver to my ear, squirming with excitement.

"Hello?" Grandma had prompted me with the right word.

"Hello, Kenny."

I was thrilled but not immediately convinced it truly was my aunt talking through the box. Her voice sounded funny. And how could it travel all the way from town?

As a boy who had gone from diapers to a child's potty and then to outdoor privies equipped with frighteningly large openings for my small bottom, I was enthralled with the farm's indoor bathroom. Grandma Schafer explained that she and Grandpa had no need for an outdoor privy, that this indoor room served the purpose. Though I was at first bewildered by the porcelain array of that regal room, the stool, sink, and bathtub, all glistening white and smooth as glass, I adapted quickly. To sit on that white oval seat and do my business and send it away in a swirl of water, leaving no residue, was a modernism to strain my comprehension. Did the mess drop into the basement? And to draw cold water, and more miraculously hot, simply by turning handles on the sink or tub, to trap it there with a plug, and to send it down the drain after washing, was reason enough for me to become, voluntarily but temporarily, the cleanest boy in South Dakota.

One evening during my first visit to that magical farm, in the spring of 1935, Aunt Ella took Mother and me to see a play presented by the Java High School senior class, a fearfully spooky performance for a three-year-old boy. Near the end of the first act, one of the characters was beheaded with a cleaver off stage (we saw victim and villain exit, heard a scream, then the cleaver's meaty thwack). Thoroughly unnerved by the sound, I nearly leaped from my seat minutes later when the murderer returned and circled the stage, displaying the severed head on a large platter. We sat fairly far back, and from that distance the illusion was startlingly convincing to my young eyes. Though I told myself trickery was involved, my heart raced. The head and platter were placed on a corner table as the scene ended. Throughout intermission I worried about that horrible head behind the purple curtain.

Grandpa and Grandma Schafer's modern farm home, 1936

To my dismay, when the curtain opened for the next act, the head and platter remained perched on the table. I was fascinated by that grisly sight, though the actors seemed to pay little attention to it. I couldn't believe their indifference. And then it happened. The head's eyes, which had been closed, suddenly opened and began looking around. My heart froze. And then the mouth opened, the lips curled back, and the teeth snapped viciously. I think I stopped breathing. Those around me, to my amazement, erupted with laughter, even Mother and Aunt Ella.

As we drove back to my grandparents' farm after the performance, Mother explained that the supposedly decapitated actor had wedged himself under the table during intermission and stuck his head through a hole in the table and platter, replacing the fake head and thus having the opportunity to ham it up for laughs, but what I had seen overpowered such logic. The severed head, mouth gaping, teeth snapping, floated above the foot of my bed on Grandma's sun porch and glared at me all through that terrible night. It repeated its levitation for nights thereafter, even when we returned to our ranch, its skin tone gradually fading to a sickly green, its stump of neck dripping blood.

In contrast to my grandparents' farmhouse, our prairie ranch home was primitive. Not only did we have no bathroom, we had no electric lights, no telephone, no running water, the norm then for rural families on the Great Plains. Our water came from an artesian well that had been dug at considerable expense for the time, one dollar a foot I later learned, and sunk 1800 feet before tapping an adequate source of water. We lugged water in from the well for cooking and for heating on the wood-burning cook stove that was fired up every day, winter and summer. A galvanized pail on a kitchen cabinet, a long-handled dipper propped inside it, provided a ready supply of drinking water. As was the custom then, we drank directly from the dipper, which served for all. We washed hands and faces in water dipped from the pail into the adjacent enameled wash basin.

Each Saturday evening and on rare special occasions, we prepared for a full bath. Mother heated two large pots of water to boiling, and Dad poured them into our large galvanized washtub. Unheated well water was added to bring the temperature down before I climbed in. I can't say I looked forward to the experience, but I complied without complaint. The corrugated bottom of the tub wasn't comfortable to sit on. I had no rubber ducky, no time for happy splashing. Mother quickly scrubbed me with a soapy washcloth, stood me up, and told me to scoot. When I scrambled out to dry, Mother slipped in; when she finished, it was Dad's turn. Our ritual ended minutes later when Dad carried the heavy tub outside and dumped the bath water behind our house.

Isolated as we were, our little flow of trivial daily incidents seemed to me as important as life itself. With little experience to numb my enthusiasm, I had not yet developed the tendency to compare, to prefer one adventure over another. I took each simple moment to be grand. Unrelated to one another, strung together like mismatched beads in a strand, our little adventures defined our time on the ranch for me and, in a small way, define me even now.

I was given almost unlimited freedom and rarely supervised. My parents trusted me to wander about on my own, to tote up my experiences, pleasant or unpleasant, and to learn from them. One day I carelessly climbed over the woven-wire fence and dropped down into the sheep pen. The clot of sheep in the pen shifted nervously, every head turned toward me. The pen, its raw ground punctured by countless small hooves and peppered with sheep droppings, would earn no seal of approval from modern mothers. Not a blade of grass grew in it. Nonetheless, I contentedly wandered around, oblivious of any danger, perfectly content to amuse myself near the fence. As I bent over to inspect an interesting stone on the ground, I was astonished to find myself suddenly airborne, sailing over the fence. After crashing to the ground outside, thoroughly spooked by my unexpected flight and rough landing, I yelped loudly. Dad rushed out from the house in time to see a lone ram trotting back to join the pack of sheep clustered on the far side of the pen. After satisfying himself that I wasn't seriously hurt, he took a pitchfork and charged into the pen, running through the scattering, bleating ewes and lambs to single out the ram that had butted me over the fence for a few sharp pokes on its haunches. Seeing the ram take his well-deserved medicine perked me up and eased my pain. I was reassured. I always would be safe when my father was near, a comforting thought because I had a nose for risky adventures.

Once, with the Fourth of July approaching, Dad brought a package of firecrackers home from Gettysburg.

"Let's shoot some off," he said.

I eagerly tailed him outside. In the late afternoon heat, Dad selected a bare spot in the yard, a patch of hard-packed earth, where he showed me how to put a firecracker on the ground and place an inverted tin can over it, leaving the fuse exposed for lighting. I liked the fizzle of the fuse, the neat way the can blasted into the air, the smell of burnt powder. After the can's bottom had been rounded out by a few explosions, Dad let me try it on my own while he watched. He walked me through the steps, giving safety instructions. I scratched a match on its box, tentatively edged flame to fuse. The match, which I held vertically down, singed my fingers. I dropped it and lit another. Backed off when the fuse spurted. The can launched into the air. Wow.

"Can I do it again?" Dad allowed a second shot. I was hooked.

Later I ended up alone in the yard with fireworks and a few wooden matches. How that happened isn't clear, though it's unlikely that Dad gave me permission to shoot them off by myself. More likely, I came across the firecrackers in the house and took things into my own hands. Whatever the reason, there I was, four years old and alone in the yard with a few Black Cats. I'd already shot a can into the air. What else could I do? For one thing, I hadn't seen the firecracker explode. The can had been in the way. Intent on discovery, I held a firecracker by the tip of its base and bent over to strike a match on a small stone. The match flared. Being an old hand at this sort of thing by now, I lit the fuse as casually as a smoker lighting a Lucky Strike. I was set to toss the firecracker away fast and observe whatever happened. Maybe I didn't see the fuse ignite. Maybe my reflexes were too slow. A sudden explosive heat tore skin from the tips of my forefinger and thumb. The event flashed past so quickly that it took seconds to feel the pain, to find my voice and bring my parents running.

Dad was furious and let me know it. Mother consoled me. Both agreed that my injury was punishment enough, that I'd surely learned my lesson. They made such decisions easily. Neither considered child-rearing complicated. They believed a parent could get along reasonably well with a measure of common sense tempered with respect for the child. Neither George nor Emma gnashed their teeth over the proper way to guide, stimulate, and prepare their children for later life. They believed that nature took care of such things if one inculcated proper moral values and taught kids the difference between right and wrong. It seemed to work. On Independence Day, when Dad shot off the rest of the firecrackers, Mother and I stood safely back, I timidly using her as a shield, peeking around her legs, my fingers still sore. But they healed without difficulty and left no scar.

A more serious accident marked me for life. One day while playing near the shack where Old Albert had lived, I studied the inviting gap beneath it. A long beam ran from end to end beneath the shack, a tempting arrangement. I climbed over the pile of debris Old Albert and others before him had tossed underneath and, with some difficulty, hoisted myself on board. Wobbling happily, I crept along the beam. Suddenly I slipped and fell. My right wrist landed on a broken Mason jar and split open. Blood spurted from the gash. Terrified by the flying blood, I scurried over the mess of cans and bottles and ran into the house, my wrist pumping spurts of red.

"What did you do?" Mother was all business, calmly asking questions while she ripped strips from an old shirt of Dad's and wrapped my wrist. I trusted her to fix the thing, but I was scared, spooked by the blood, trembling. The kitchen floor was slick beneath us by the time she slowed the tide and called to Dad, who fortunately was in the barn and not away from the ranch. We piled into the Model A pickup truck and headed for Gettysburg. I sat on Mother's lap, watching blood seep through the cloth even though she pressed firmly on my wrist. Dad, with an eye on the oozing blood dripping onto Mother's dress, whipped the pickup truck over the dirt country roads, raising great clouds of dust.

In the physician's office, the doctor misjudged me and attempted to lull me into submitting to his anesthetic by pretending he had a piece of candy for me. What did he take me for? When his foolish ploy failed, he switched to force and tried to ram his ether mask over my face. I fought him, standing upright on his narrow operating table, blood spraying and spattering him and me until Dad weighed in and locked me in his arms.

When I awoke my wrist was neatly wrapped in white gauze, not a speck of blood visible. The doctor smiled and handed me a piece of candy as we left his office, telling me not to eat it until Mother gave the okay. Our Model A stirred up little dust on our leisurely drive home. My wound probably had begun to smart by then but I remember no pain. From this adventure I carry a rough, inverted V that stretches along my inner right wrist. It's not among the finest cosmetic scars I've seen, but the good

25

country doctor accomplished what he needed to do: stop the bleeding and close the wound.

When I studied anatomy years later, I learned the name of the artery sliced open by the jagged Mason jar. My ulnar artery. When severed, this artery pumps blood from both proximal and distal ends because it connects through branches in the hand with its partner on the opposite side of the wrist, the radial artery. No wonder my mother had difficulty controlling the bleeding, even when pressing firmly on the cloth around my wrist. She probably pressed, as one often is taught to do, on the artery above the cut, on the side nearest the heart, a maneuver that slowed but didn't completely stop my hemorrhaging. Had my father been away from the ranch, had he and the Model A not been within hailing distance and available to drive me to town for immediate treatment, I might easily have drawn my last breath as a youngster in my mother's arms.

Dad taught me about guns on the sheep ranch. I was with him one spring afternoon on the edge of the field some distance north of our house when he shot a rabbit with his single-shot 12-gauge. The rabbit had been intended for supper, but it had flushed only a few yards away, and Dad, uncharacteristically impatient, had fired too quickly, blasting the animal at close range. The concentrated charge of pellets blew open the rabbit's chest and sent a spray of fur, blood, and muscle flying. The heart, which miraculously escaped injury, lay fully exposed and continued to beat. We bent over the rabbit as it lay deathly still, its eyes unseeing, its flesh unsalvageable. Small bits of tissue and bloody fur clung to blades of grass on one side. And in the rabbit's gaping chest the exposed heart pumped briskly and glistened in the sun.

The little heart puzzled me.

"Is he dead?" I asked.

"Yes." Dad took the spent shell from his gun and tossed it to the ground. I picked it up to sniff the burnt gunpowder.

"But his heart's still going. How can it do that? And go so fast?" I was fascinated by the sight, considered it curious, not grisly.

"It just does."

The answer satisfied me. "Does my heart look like that?"

"Yours is bigger. It doesn't go so fast."

A pool of blood collected around the heart. The little dynamo, withering and nearly empty, chugged away, unstoppable. Even as we drove off the heart beat on.

Some two decades later, for a student laboratory experiment, I opened the plastron of an anesthetized turtle and isolated its beating heart. As I ligated key vessels and attached recording devices, my turtle heart alternately compressed itself and relaxed, cycling sluggishly but reliably, an apt machine that I knew would perform as required, would rev up or slow down when I stimulated its nerves, or flooded it with neurotransmitters. On other laboratory benches around me were similar turtle hearts, each one squeezing itself together, relaxing, squeezing again, doggedly maintaining its slow rhythm. Many of my classmates were agog, and unsure of the resilience of those self-starting engines. To me it was old news. I had come to appreciate the ruggedness of the heart much earlier, as a four-year-old boy on the edge of a remote Dakota field, held spellbound by a dead rabbit's heart that refused to stop. A heart that pumped briskly and glistened in the sun.

As I had on the day Dad shot the rabbit, I often rode along with him in the Model A pickup. I'm not sure who owned the vehicle. It may have been ours. It may have come with the job on the ranch. Either way, it was ours to use. Once, not long after we had arrived on the ranch, I even used it myself. It came about when Dad and our collie, Pal, rounded up the sheep in the south pasture for shearing. I sat beside Dad as he drove the pickup behind the skittering flock in a zig-zag pattern, nudging them toward the pen. The sheep were unruly and kept doubling back behind us. Pal did his best to turn the tide. But while he snarled and nipped the haunches of escapees on one side of the flock, others broke loose from the opposite side. Coverage on both flanks was needed.

"We need help," Dad said, looking at me.

As much as I'd have liked to help, I knew I was too slow for the job. Besides, I had already demonstrated that I was of a size that made my backside a tantalizing target for renegade rams. I wasn't eager to be tattooed again. But Dad had another job in mind.

"Can you drive this thing?" he asked.

Without waiting for my answer, he put the pickup in low gear and adjusted the accelerator lever on the steering column to move the truck along at the speed of a man walking. He then opened the driver's door and stepped out on the running board with his left foot, making room for me to scoot over behind the steering wheel. By now it had soaked in that he wasn't kidding. He really wanted me to drive the thing. I was three old, and enormously excited by the opportunity.

While keeping a firm hand on the steering wheel, Dad propped me up on my knees and had me grip the wheel. Then he edged around the open door and, from his perch on the running board, slammed the door shut while controlling the steering wheel through the open window.

"Okay," he said, "Take over." He released the steering wheel.

The huge wheel was a load, but I managed to twist it from side to side under Dad's prompting. Admittedly, there wasn't much to it, but I imagined it to be a gigantic enterprise. Dad seemed satisfied that I could keep the old truck on a reasonable course, and, after warning me to avoid all rocks, he hopped off the running board and ran ahead to attend to one of the flanks, leaving me higher than the clouds but a bit nervous.

I guided that old black pickup over the uneven prairie, trailing Dad and Pal and the sheep, angling a little to the right, then to the left, the engine throttled back and moving us slowly, steadily along. Not able to see over the hood very well, I banged over several cantaloupe-sized stones with a jerk and a lurch but wasn't overly concerned. The bumps added spice to the ride. I soon got the feel of the wheel and relaxed, even ad-libbed. I twisted the wheel hard to the left and curled the pickup into a tight circle. After one revolution I made another. Watching the horizon slowly spin, I couldn't have felt more self-important had I been maneuvering a battleship. When I came out of the second turn, I spotted Dad hurrying my way. Rather than take a third loop, as I had intended, I straightened the wheel and aimed for the center of the flock. Dad grinned, with relief I suppose, and went back to dealing with the strays.

Thus we proceeded across the prairie, a disorderly flock of sheep leading the way, man and collie trailing on the flanks, and, in the rear, a boy in a meandering black Model A pickup, certain he was the focal point of the universe. When we neared our destination, I began to worry, wondering how I would stop the thing. Wondering whether I would I be able to make it through the gate. It didn't occur to me that I could circle in a holding pattern near the pen, or, more to the point, that my father would look out for me, or at least for the truck. With Pal's help, he had herded the sheep into the pen and closed the gate well before I rolled into the danger zone. He jumped aboard and took over, giving me a gentle pat on the back as I slid over to the right. For months, even years afterward, whenever I thought of my experimental circles on the prairie, I puffed up. And why not? I had driven a pickup all by myself.

On our isolated ranch I rarely saw anyone but my parents, a situation that gradually transformed my earlier genial interest in strangers to a shy timidity. The rare visitor coming to the ranch, even the occasional relative I hadn't often seen, became an instant threat. Intruders terrified me, not because I feared they would harm me, but because I felt uncomfortable in their presence. One day Aunt Katherine, one of Dad's sisters and Mother's best friend in high school, came unexpectedly for a visit. I heard her car drive up, a sound easily detected amid the silence of the prairie, and peeked out the kitchen window to see who it was. Recognizing my aunt, I scrambled off to hide, a nervous mouse ducking into his hole.

"Aunt Katherine's here," Mother called.

I hunkered down in the farthest corner under my crib and shivered as I heard footsteps coming. I tried to be as quiet as my shadow and vowed to come out only after my aunt had gone away.

"Come and say hello to Aunt Katherine," Mother said, bending down to peer at me.

"No. I don't want to."

Mother wasn't swayed by my rude reply. She ordered me out and marched me into our small living room. Aunt Katherine, cloaked in a faint cloud of perfume, hugged me enthusiastically. I held my arms at my side.

"You're getting so big, Kenny."

I knew better. I was quite small. And I wasn't much for small talk. I retreated and stood behind Mother, too bashful to utter a word. When the two friends began chattering away, I slipped away, relieved to be alone again.

When viewed from today's world of instant communications, our isolation on that ranch is difficult to imagine. No radio, no newspaper, no telephone. Only rare contact with neighbors and townsmen. Thus, splendidly exiled, I passed through my key developmental years with little intellectual stimulation beyond the simple lessons Mother taught me. That remote setting, by default, became my primitive kindergarten. It was a sorry place to prepare myself for battle with the explosion in technology in the latter half of the Twentieth Century, but it had its compensations.

In that sky-dominated land, the sun became my clock and my calendar. One who lives on the prairie cannot fail to notice the sun's daily arc, its northerly and southerly wanderings through the seasons, the shifting shadows on the ground. I often played on the north side of our house, where shadows stretched and shortened with the seasons. In winter I played in snowy shadows there, in summer in the sun. Being outside nearly every day under that broad sky, usually for hours at a time, I learned instinctively how little heat the low winter sun threw, how hot the high summer sun. Such things were as evident as the force of Dakota winds. Like our sheep, I accepted whatever temperature came, bundling up against the chilling bite of winter, running nearly naked in summer heat.

In winter I saw the ewes' bellies swelling, because, Dad explained, lambs were growing inside them. In early spring the lambs made their way out under my knowing eyes. Even the occasional ewe waddling through the pen with a lamb's head protruding from its rear end raised no more than passing interest. That was the way things were, just as the steps of newborn lambs were loose-jointed, wobbly. After lambing season the pastures greened, wild flowers budded, and the sheep grazed low through the grass, their teeth brushing the earth. In late May, I watched carefully as the shearers came to clip our cash crop. After we had collected the sheep into their pen, the men pulled them out in turn and forced them down, clipping off their woolly coats with hand-powered shears that clicked incessantly.

The abrupt change in the sheep amazed me. The once-rotund animals were transformed into pathetically skinny creatures, their rib cages prominent, their legs mere spindles, their heads suddenly too large for their bodies. The shearers stuffed the wool into huge burlap sacks, each one taller than a man, then loaded the sacks into their truck and hauled the wool away, to be made into coats and pants, my mother said.

Death was common in our life. I once threw a hateful glare at a mangy coyote as it ripped its fangs into the mangled carcass of a fallen lamb. Dad and I chased the beast with the pickup truck and saw it hole up. He dug it out and, as it raced away, blasted it with his shotgun. Good, I thought as the predator fell; he would eat no more lambs. I felt no pity for the captured mice and fledgling meadowlarks our cats teased and played with before they ate them, though I hated the hawks that swooped on our few baby chicks and carried them away gripped in their talons.

I heard no music, saw no art, knew only the common sounds and scenes of prairie life: the fluted warble of meadowlarks, the metallic trill of red-winged blackbirds, the surging leaps of jackrabbits, the softness of moonlight, the brilliance of stars undimmed by man-made light.

We were largely self-sufficient, producing most of what we ate, potatoes, beans, corn, lettuce, radishes, chicken, beef and pork. We rarely ate mutton. I absorbed small lessons useful in a rural environment, observing Dad milk our lone cow, watching chicks hatch from their eggs, or, more often, removing from the nests fresh eggs for frying while nervously warding off the sharp beaks of maternal-minded hens. I helped my mother put seeds in the ground and collect pitiful vegetables from the poor dry soil to be cooked for supper or preserved in Mason jars. Our grocery shopping targeted mainly staples such as flour, seasonings, and coffee.

We slaughtered animals as needed. When our chicks had grown into spring fryers, Mother butchered them one by one for Sunday meals, chopping off their heads with a hatchet. The headless fowl amazed me, leaping wildly, blood gushing from their necks, wings flapping, seemingly more alive, if only temporarily, than they had been with heads intact. After they bled themselves out, Mother dipped them in a pail of scalding water and plucked their feathers before removing their entrails. I detested the smell of scalded feathers but loved what followed: the wonderful aroma of chicken frying in the pan, the delicate taste of Mother's spring fryers.

Converting larger animals to food took more effort. I remember my father slaughtering a hog, and later a yearling steer. The steer stood calmly near the barn, chewing his cud and facing Dad and his .22 rifle. Dad approached to about ten feet away, aimed between the animal's eyes, elevated a couple of inches above that, and fired. The steer collapsed without a sound save for the thump of his trunk meeting earth. Butchering of the steer consumed most of the day, the two men adroitly skinning, slicing, and carving up the beef.

The hog didn't go quietly. Dad had no bullets for his rifle on that day, a few weeks after we had moved to the ranch. He and Uncle Fred herded the hog, which weighed a couple hundred pounds, into the barn and closed the door. Then they shooed him into a small pen, their plan being to corner the hog and knock him out with a blow to the head by a sturdy ball-peen hammer. After much maneuvering to corner the skittish hog, Dad planted himself and gave a mighty swing. It landed off center. The hog, hurt and enraged but fully conscious, squealed and scrambled around the small pen, his cries reverberating from the barn's rafters and walls like the clamor of dozens of pigs in peril. George and Fred tried to grab the hog and restrain it, but strong as they were, they were no match for the hard-charging hog.

Peering through the slats of the pen, I felt my heart racing, sensed the tension mount among all four of us,. No one liked the primitive battle, the hog least of all. But the ultimate outcome was never in doubt. When the breathless hog stopped his wild circling to collect himself, panting loudly, Dad struck again, this time accurately. The hog collapsed, unconscious. I was glad it was over. The men quickly hoisted the hog by his hind legs with a block and tackle and slashed his throat to drain his blood. They proceeded methodically, expertly, with the ritual of butchering they had learned while young from their own father. They chatted amiably as they sliced out slabs for bacon, shoulders for ham. While they trimmed out roasts and chops, they brought me into the process, informing me what they were doing on the assumption, I suppose, that one day I would take up their role. I watched with keen interest, especially when they cleaned the intestines, pulling them inside out and scraping off the inner layers to leave only the glistening translucent casing that Dad later stuffed with the sausage he made, a savory concoction ground with our small hand grinder and spiced with handfuls of seasonings. Most of the meat was canned or smoked to preserve it. We had no refrigerator or freezer.

Despite the scarcity of money, my parents and I made one magnificent evening foray into Gettysburg. Perhaps there was a reason for celebration, a birthday, or an anniversary. Whatever the reason, we took in a show, our word for a movie. The film long ago threaded itself into oblivion, but what we did afterward gleams yet with the brightness of a full moon overhead. We stopped for a luscious treat, strawberry sundaes, in a nearly empty restaurant, the only time I remember the three of us going out for something to eat. The one we invaded in Gettysburg was bright, its ceiling lights glaring on off-white walls. At the late hour the restaurant was nearly empty. We three sat around a small square table, waiting for our ice cream, speaking in soft whispers. I was the first to spot the waitress bringing her tray with the fancy clear-glass dishes, each filled with a large scoop of vanilla, a circle of red around it, and crowned with a puff of whipped cream and a whole strawberry. Dad got the biggest strawberry. I scooped my spoon into the frozen treat and caught a chunk of berry. Life had never been sweeter.

Only one adventure on the ranch ranked higher than our night on the town, that a trip to a neighboring farm. Dad invited me to ride with him late one afternoon. As we approached our destination, I saw a large silo looming over the barn. Most farms in the region didn't have a silo, so I knew this was a special farm, a prosperous one. Dad pulled into the farm yard and stopped some distance from the house. The farmer came outside to greet us. Dad stepped down from the pickup and rested one foot on the running board while he and the farmer talked. I studied the imposing silo.

And then I caught sight of her, a raven-haired creature nearly my age standing in the doorway of the farm house. She ventured out onto the stoop. I climbed down from the pickup and stood waiting, watching her come shyly toward me.

"Hello," I said, striving to sound grown up, awed by her angelic appearance.

"Hello." Her voice was less serious, more a happy giggle.

I cannot recall a word beyond our greeting. What I remember is our hesitation, our feet working the ground like nervous colts. I was taken by her, thoroughly infatuated by her demure smile and curious gaze, which I took as a sign of her interest in me. Being naively assured of our common bond, and already a planner, I edged a half-step closer and imagined our future. I would visit her farm over the years. We would become good friends. We would grow up together, very likely marry. A new thrill filled my chest, a feathery rush beneath my ribs.

I don't know how long the dark-haired moppet and I fidgeted and talked. Five minutes? Fifteen? However long it was, the interval persists to this moment. When Dad broke the spell and called me into the pickup, I stepped in smartly, thinking the girl would notice how well I behaved, even as my spirits plunged. I waved once through the side window and turned to face straight ahead, impersonating a brave soldier departing but aching as we drove away. For weeks afterward I impatiently awaited our next trip to the farm with the silo, longing to see my young friend again. I thought of what we would talk about, what secrets I would tell her. I pictured her giggling, confiding her secrets to me. But it was a pipe dream induced by innocence and rudely interrupted by forces beyond our control. I never returned to that farm with a silo. I never saw the raven-haired girl again.

Those years weren't favorable for sheep ranchers in the Dakotas. With rain as scarce as our Depression dollars, the Great Plains choked on a severe drought. According to most sources, the notorious Dust Bowl of the 1930s didn't extend as far north as South Dakota. Nebraska, Kansas, Oklahoma, and Texas were said to be even more parched. Maybe so, but we were dry enough for me.

Powerful winds move freely across the plains, much as they do at sea. In the dry 1930s prairie winds lifted plowed land desiccated to dust and whirled it hundreds of feet into the air, blotting out the sun and swirling in thick, oppressive clouds that raced over the land. The dark storms lasted at times for days. Surely tons of Nebraska and Kansas dirt blew across the ranch, contributing their bulk to the black blizzards that clamped visibility like an inky midnight fog. When the suffocating storms hit in daytime, Mother put a lantern in our kitchen window, a beacon to guide Dad back through the blackness to the house. When he emerged from the suffocating storm, Dad's eyelids were rimmed in black with dirt swept from his eyes by constant blinking. After he took off his cap and the large handkerchief he wore to protect nose and mouth, I told him he looked like a robber wearing a mask of black dirt. When the wind finally collapsed, heavy dark lines of dirt streaked the land. Thicker drifts collected along fences sometimes completely covering the posts and woven wire and allowing sheep to step over the buried fence and escape from their pasture. In our house, the heavy swirls of powdery dust blown in through cracks yielded to Mother's broom.

Near the end of our stay on the ranch, Dad took extra work to supplement his meager wage. In the morning he set out with his black metal lunch bucket filled with sandwiches and dill pickles, a thermos of hot coffee stored in its top half, and tramped across the prairie to the southeast. I had no recollection of what he did, where he worked, but a recent visit to the area and a conversation with one of our former neighbors, who still lives on his family farm, provided a likely answer.

"He probably worked on Cottonwood Lake," Robert (Bud) Merrill said. "Practically every man in the area helped build the Cottonwood dam. It was a WPA project." Bud Merrill was a school boy when my family lived on the sheep ranch, the Merrills being our nearest neighbors, their farm less than a mile east of our ranch, a place I recall once visiting. And, remarkably, Bud Merrill said he remembered me, the little boy from those distant days, a revelation that surprised and pleased me.

"I suppose your dad caught a ride to the lake somewhere along the road, probably with someone driving a team of horses. If not, he walked about five miles to get there."

Dad didn't keep that job long. The owner of our ranch, Mr. Gidley, died in September of 1937. With the future of the ranch uncertain, Dad decided to look elsewhere for work. My parents held urgent discussions. What would they do? Jobs were scarce. They had a son - and a baby on the way. Where would they find shelter? Money to live on?

We drove one day to an uninhabited farm some distance away. The farm house, square and two stories high, stood tall south of the country road. An impressive pane of stained glass decorated its front door. The upstairs bedrooms were spacious, the stairway just what a boy needed for climbing. I was ready to move in. But the house was the only good thing about the place. The stingy owner's deal was too severe, the farm machinery in bad repair. Dad would have none of it. He would search further.

I had noticed Mother's middle growing larger. I thought I knew what that meant. I'd seen plenty of swollen sheep and cows and mother cats and knew about things growing inside them. Mother and I talked. Before long, she told me, I would have a brother or a sister. I was thrilled. I would have someone to play with. Giddy with happiness, I went to the north kitchen window and looked out, thinking of the baby soon to join us.

I noticed a clump of tumbleweeds entangled along the fence. More continued to gather there as I watched, blown by a brisk southwestern wind. Soon the clump grew so large that the fence could hold no more. Newcomers began to roll over the wedge-shaped barrier and clear the fence and tumble on. I liked the way the clever tumbleweeds found their way over the fence and happily bounced as they traveled onward. Then I thought again of the baby growing inside Mother. Before me was a scene of great beauty and interest, but my expected brother or sister would never see it. The clever tumbleweeds would tumble on, never to return, never to cross this fence again. My happiness turned to grief. Bitter tears came. I was five years old. I had begun to realize that human lives overlap imperfectly.

My first sister was born late in 1937. Shortly before she gave birth, Mother traveled to spend her confinement with her parents on their wonderfully modern farm. I went along to be with her and my grandparents over the holidays. One night, on December 29th, I awoke in my bed on the sun porch and heard Mother's desperate cries coming from one of the bedrooms. Aunt Katherine, the one I'd hidden from on the ranch, was in attendance. She was a nurse but had no analgesic available. Mother's cries of pain grew louder.

The doctor arrived minutes before the crucial moment. Soon I heard a baby crying. After the room had been tidied up, I was invited in to see our new family member. The bedroom was remarkably bright, illuminated by one of those magical electric lights centered on the ceiling. And in the bed, beside Mother, lay my baby sister, a sleeping creature much tinier than I had expected. Mother told me her name. Carol Ann.

The attending doctor, before he left, gave me a gift, a small pocket knife. It was, I believed, a sign of my growing up, of becoming a big boy. One could do many things with a pocket knife. I explored the ways.

"Did you do this?" my furious mother asked a few days later, pointing to the floor under a rocking chair in the corner of the living room. The floor was covered with an attractive linoleum, quite new and patterned with a mosaic of complex squares. I gazed at the spot my mother pointed to. Someone had carved three letters in the linoleum under the chair, a place not easily seen. I was five-years-old, soon to be six. It seemed senseless to issue a denial. The initials, KLG, matched my own.

About the time of Carol's birth, we left the sheep ranch for a farm Dad had found north of Gettysburg. We arrived with little enthusiasm and stayed only several months, a time I've mostly forgotten. An old phonograph had been left in one of the bedrooms, a relic abandoned by the former occupants. I amused myself by winding it up and playing the few scratchy records stored inside. I disliked the tinny sounds it produced, the tremulous voice of someone with a register between male and female. Nonetheless, I toyed with it from time to time because I was fascinated that a machine could produce speech from a heavy arm and needle gliding on a spinning black record. I had not yet been introduced to a radio.

A couple of snapshots taken of me on that farm survive. In both I'm dressed as a cowboy. In one I stand with the vast open land behind me, Pal nuzzling me. In another I sit on a placid horse, the reins of his bridle dangling to the ground. My cowboy outfit had been a Christmas present from Santa Claus, complete with black hat, neckerchief, vest, and chaps. Mom and Dad had splurged and added a pistol that shot suction-tipped darts, a tin target with a big bulls-eye, and a belt with holster. I had everything a cowboy needed. Cowboys were great. I intended to be one someday.

Kenneth and Pal, 1938

When we vacated the sheep ranch, we had to leave some of our household goods behind. Dad didn't return to the ranch to pick them up until the weather warmed early the next spring. He was too late. Someone had cleaned out the house. Mother's cherished memento from her childhood, an elegant China doll, was missing, as were some furniture and dishes, but, as Aunt Ella told me, "It wasn't a big loss. You folks didn't have much to lose."

The loss simplified our next move. Dad had fewer goods to load onto the truck he borrowed. After about six months on the place north of Gettysburg, my parents gave up on arid farming and sought a better life in the nearby town of Onida. It was the summer of 1938.

CHAPTER 3

Some weeks before we arrived in Onida, President Roosevelt signed the Fair Labor Standards Act, a law which among its provisions established a minimum wage, forty cents an hour. Had Dad been so lushly rewarded for his Onida labors, we might have fried a steak now and then. But as with most of what Washington cobbles together, the details of the law mocked its high-sounding name. It applied only to businesses involved in interstate commerce and meant nothing to most Americans, my father included, who signed on with the Works Projects Administration and dug ditches for forty dollars a month. The WPA nourished us in its fashion. In fact, the availability of WPA jobs had been the lure that drew our family to Onida.

Onida is a typical Dakota small town. Lying roughly thirty miles east of the wide Missouri, and squarely in the center of Sully County, Onida buzzed with about six hundred residents when we arrived. As the only settlement in the county other than minuscule Agar nine miles to the north, Onida serves as the

43

county seat for an area that encompasses roughly a thousand square miles. Most of this land is as devoid of humans as the deserted Gidley sheep ranch, part of which lay within the northern edge of the county. On average, Sully County is home to about two people per square mile.

After our isolated existence on ranch and farm, Onida loomed as a metropolis to my unseasoned eyes. Being suddenly surrounded by clusters of strangers marked an abrupt change in my life, but I adapted quickly to the congestion. What bothered me was the commodities. Beyond Dad's WPA salary, our family was eligible to receive surplus staples, a helpful boost to our table but an embarrassment to me. Even at age six I saw the government food as a demeaning stigma, a handout for those unable to make it on their own. Mother assigned me to collect our allotments from the central distribution point, a storage building near the county court house. I resisted. Mother insisted, quietly but firmly, leaving no way for me to wiggle out of the chore.

When I set out on my mission with my empty little wagon, I furtively glanced around to see if anyone noticed me. Onida's court house anchors the northern end of Main Street, but I avoided the main drag. I pulled my wagon along the side streets where there was less likelihood of being seen. And while loading the potatoes, rice, flour, prunes, or dried beans into my wagon, I kept my eyes down, feeling uncomfortable even among the other unfortunates who collected their rations as I collected ours. I wish I knew the source of my acute sensitivity when so young. Perhaps I sensed a kindred embarrassment in my mother.

Now far removed from that situation, I see it differently, see no stigma in the free food. Dad's labor easily earned his meager salary and the surplus commodities. I went to watch him work at times, saw him and other men active in their long ditch, ventured close to watch the blur of shovels, to smell the freshly dug sweet earth - the acrid manly sweat. I saw no leaning on long handles. Those men moved dirt. Standing shoulder deep in the long ditch, the under-arms of their shirts soaked, the dried edges white with salt, they fired endless volleys onto the growing mound that paralleled the ditch. Dad worked fluidly, repetitively, putting his head, shoulders, and shovel down, stepping on the shovel to drive it deep into the dirt, leaning back and twisting his shoulders to complete the loading, then straightening up and deftly flinging another clump onto the mound. He gave me a wink and a smile without breaking his rhythm. His was honest labor, a respectable way to earn our bread.

Befitting our income, we rented a tiny house in Onida, its flaking paint weathered to a dull white. A narrow corridor inside the west wall served as our kitchen; it had a cold-water tap, cupboards, a narrow counter top, and a small walk-in pantry. We added a kerosine cook stove and placed a small table in front of the single window facing west. The pantry was the size of a telephone booth and dark as a tomb inside. Mother once stuffed me in there for a misbehavior I've forgotten and locked the hasp. The terrifying darkness unnerved me. I pounded the door and screamed my apologies in the long minute before she released me. Although my mother was a gentle women, not given to raising her voice, she believed it her God-given duty to do right, not wrong. The only course of action acceptable for her, and for her children, was the Bible-sanctioned right way. Her children would obey her and respect her, or else.

Whether from my lesson in the pantry or not, I tend to become uneasy in close confinement, a quirk that surfaced not long after Mother had imprisoned me in the darkness. Three new acquaintances and I discovered a stack of corrugated metal culverts beside the nearby railroad tracks. The culverts were long enough to span beneath a rural highway, and of a diameter that a small boy could crawl into and wriggle through, as my companions did one by one. Wary of the enterprise, I was the last to try it. My heart pounded as I ducked my head in, then grudgingly brought in shoulders and the rest of me. About a third of the way through I was suddenly trapped, wedged tightly by shrinking metal, a terrifying illusion apparently brought on when I nervously tried to speed up by crawling on my hands and knees and found myself locked in place. Paralyzed with fear, a timeless interval passed before I discovered I could edge forward by flattening out and slithering on my belly. I forced myself to lie flat and snaked my way with excruciating slowness toward the distant circle of daylight. The culvert squeezed on me. Fighting panic, I wriggled and twisted but made little progress. I gasped for breath. Would I never escape? What if someone blocked the ends? Hours later, or so it seemed, my head finally inched out of the long confining space.

Carol, who was about six months old when we moved to town, slept in her baby buggy in the bedroom with our parents. I slept in the living room on our fold-down couch, a cozy arrangement for all. With our three tiny rooms, and an outhouse in back, we had all the essentials.

The couch I slept on survives in a photograph taken soon after we arrived in Onida. An itinerant photographer came to our door, offering inexpensive portraits. Mother proudly chose to pose her baby. She propped Carol up on the couch as I looked on, the photographer coaxed a pleasant expression, the instant was captured. That portrait survives as the only tangible reminder I have of those distant, innocent days, of that tiny house that sheltered us.

Carol in late 1938

On a bright morning in the fall of 1938, a day remarkably sharp in memory, I enrolled in the first grade. I see the route I followed as I trudged eastward on that opening day of school, eager to begin, full of excitement yet apprehensive. I knew practically no one in town. Mother had volunteered to accompany me when she tucked in my polo shirt and adjusted the suspenders on my wash pants. But I chose to go alone.

"Be a good boy," she admonished as I left. I merged with a stream of boys and girls, strangers every one, that flowed with much jabbering into the elementary school and churned along the lower central hallway. I asked for directions. The first grade, an older girl told me, met in the room on the south side, the second grade in the one to the north. Older kids went upstairs. I walked into the room on the south side and transformed myself into a school boy.

That evening my parents questioned me.

"Who is your teacher?" Mother asked.

"Miss Durie."

"Your teacher is a man?" Dad said. Both look surprised.

"No." How could they imagine that Miss Durie was a man? It took us a moment to sort it out. At age six I considered words to be useful tools, nothing more. Admittedly, I had enjoyed the rhythm of nursery rhymes, but the stories told by the rhymes interested me far more than their sounds. Dylan Thomas once claimed that as a youngster he loved the words alone of nursery rhymes, the sounds they made, the "colours" they cast on his eyes, that he didn't much care what the words said. I leaned to the opposite, no budding poet I. I saw words in black and white and cared little how my teacher's name sounded in my ear. What intrigued me was the confusion three syllables could create.

School was pleasant, logical. Mother's tutoring had prepared me well and put me ahead of most of my classmates. I enjoyed our simple lessons, our teacher, our recesses where we flew on giant swings or ran aimlessly through the school yard. I had no aspirations, no goals, yet even then I held the conceit that someday I would - for lack of a more precise goal - be successful. Where this unwarranted optimism came from, I cannot say. But my confidence that I would rise above the conditions of my young life was as solid as the ground beneath me, and as unshakable. I never doubted. And this deep conviction, I think, was the factor that sustained me when we hit rough times.

School formed itself into a pattern of small desks lined in neat rows, a small body for each desk. Stored within my desk were my thin school books, a tablet of lined white paper, a few sharp-tipped pencils, a gum eraser, and a tiny box of crayons. Our exercises were as routine as the sunrise. I nodded as Miss Durie wrote numbers on the black board. I read *See Dick. See Dick run. See Dick jump. See Jane.* I constructed crude shapes from sheets of heavy paper and applied my crayons to them. I behaved. I remembered what my teacher said, mastered what my simple books contained. I never exerted myself, didn't need to. School required no effort and I gave none, a pattern that was to continue for the next thirteen years. In my ignorance I imagined I was learning all I needed to know. I thought I was quite smart. Dad noticed my cockiness.

"Bet you don't know which is heavier," he said. "A pound of feathers or a pound of bones."

Did he think I was stupid? I knew about feathers and bones. Everyone did. "A pound of bones," I said, not concealing my smugness.

"Wrong."

Wrong? I wasn't wrong. "I know a pound of bones is..." Wait a minute. A pound of...he'd set a trap and I'd jumped right into it. Maybe I still had a thing or two to learn.

I did no reading outside of school, never considered it. We had no books at home, only the family Bible. No newspapers. One didn't buy reading material when one lacked more basic items. Recognition of my mammoth waste, the squandering of those precious years when the brain is most absorbent and retentive, would come later. I didn't fritter away those years intentionally. I simply knew no better.

When Halloween arrived in Onida, there was no talk of trick-or-treating, no knocking on doors, no being bought off with candy or other treats. Night mischief was expected. Young kids streaked windows of houses and cars with bars of soap. Older kids, and young men, tipped over outhouses. Dad predicted ours would topple during the night. It did. As did practically every one in town. One man had loudly proclaimed that his privy wouldn't be touched, that he would stand guard inside with a shotgun. Under cover of darkness some stout fellows approached his yard stealthily, and, on signal, gave a mighty shove, tipping the outhouse door-side down. As the footsteps raced away, the trapped man stuck his head through one of the suddenly-created oval windows and yelped loudly for help. Even had the opening been larger, he would not have attempted unaided escape.

Soon we were into winter, my favorite season then. I loved the snow, dug tunnels in it, blasted my overshoes through undisturbed patches while making my way to and from school morning, noon, and evening. Lunch wasn't served in our school. We walked home to eat. One day a severe blizzard struck the town, the snow falling heavily when I awakened that morning. Six or more inches covered the ground by noontime, with deeper drifts blown by the wind. As we were dismissed for lunch (we were expected back for our afternoon classes), I found myself face-to-face with my father in the hallway, schoolmates all around. Dad had brought a sandwich for me in his old black lunch pail, hot cocoa in his thermos, all prepared by Mother. He wore an old sheepskin coat, a cap with the earflaps down, worn gloves. His eyebrows and eyelashes were streaked with snow, his face blotchy-red from the cold. He had come to me in kindness, a thoughtful father, to save me from walking in the brutal weather.

And I? An ungrateful lout. Suddenly embarrassed, and wishing he hadn't come, I wanted him to vanish. I was ashamed of him. Was it his clothing? His coat was old, his earflaps unfashionable. Or his station? My classmates knew whose fathers worked for the WPA and whose had real jobs. Surely Dad sensed what I felt, but he gave no sign of it. I grabbed his lunch pail and hurried him to the door. I waved with relief as he turned up his collar and went out into the cold swirling snow. That brief incident quickly faded and lay dormant for over a decade, not recalled until shortly after Dad's death, too late to make amends. Looking back to that stormy day, shamed by my inexplicable haughtiness, I can't imagine who I thought I was.

Another embarrassment, one that struck the following spring, soon turned to rage. Mother sent me to pick up our monthly allotment of commodities from the distribution point. I loaded my wagon and reluctantly wheeled along Main Street to buy the loaf of bread Mother wanted from the grocery. Nearing home, I passed the home of one of my classmates. Jerry was playing with two other boys on the lawn. The trio inspected my load of commodities and bread and found it quite humorous. Their families brought food home from the grocery in their cars.

"I didn't know you got bread with your commodities," Jerry said. He snatched up the loaf and tossed it to one of his friends, intending to play keep-away. I took the bait and rushed from one to the other as they gleefully lobbed the loaf around. The end of the wrapper broke and slices spilled out. One of them took a bite from a slice, then sailed it away.

"Good bread," he said. Another bit into another slice and pronounced it "yummy." I chased the shrinking loaf, seething as it flew from one to another. By the time I salvaged the bread only a third of it remained. I dared my tormentors to try to get it back, to sink their ugly teeth in one more slice. How could anyone, even a stupid kid, intentionally waste food? When I reached home, I was in tears, aching for revenge. I knew Dad would march up there and teach those young morons a lesson. But he disappointed me. He and Mother accepted the loss far better than I. Confused by their unexpected capitulation, feeling sorry for myself, I screamed at them. Had I done something so destructive, so stupid, wouldn't they have swooped down on me?

Why were they willing to let other kids get away with insulting me, insulting them?

Though I developed a mild sense of inferiority because of our limited means, I was generally happy during the two years we spent in Onida. I had several good friends, Owen, another Jerry, and Bob, among others. We played games with larger groups: hide and seek, kick the can, run sheep run. We roamed the town grinning. I had a prized possession, an air rifle given to me as a Christmas present by my parents. Though tin cans were my favorite target, I wasn't above shooting a few sparrows. Our neighbor to the south had a garage with a square window composed of four separate panes. It wasn't an errant shot that plinked the center of the lower right pane, leaving a small cone-shaped hole, a defect the owner surely noticed, though he never identified the marksman.

It was in Onida that I saw the first cracks in our family appear. While we were on the ranch, and later on the farm north of Gettysburg, Dad was almost always home in the evening. But in Onida he began to slip out after supper, bound for the pool hall to play cards and drink beer. I paid little attention to the change until the evening he prowled from room to room, rummaging through closets, opening cupboards, looking into covered dishes. I had never seen him so agitated. Mother and I sat on the couch in the living room.

"Where is it?" he said, making his way back to the bedroom.

Mother bent forward, her elbows on her knees, and buried her face in her hands. She did not answer.

"Where is it?" His words were angrier this time, hard edged. Dad stood in the bedroom doorway, Mother's purse open in his hands.

She began to sob. He stormed into the kitchen.

"What does he want?" I whispered.

"I put away a five-dollar bill for groceries, and he wants it to play cards."

I didn't understand. Why would Dad use our food money to play cards with? Why would he be so stupid? And why was he acting so mean? Making Mother cry. He rattled dishes in the cupboards. It made me angry.

"Where did you put it?" I asked.

She pointed to the floor. I didn't understand, gave her a puzzled look.

"It's in my shoe."

I studied her worn lace-up shoes and felt a little better. What a neat hiding place. Dad would never find the money. But he didn't give up. He prowled from room to room, searching, growling, badgering, swearing. Mother cried, took more heat. I was mad at Dad. Afraid of him. At last Mother gave in. She took off her shoe and handed him the bill. When he dashed off to the pool hall like a man running to catch a train, we were glad to see him, but not the five dollars, go. I don't recall, maybe never knew, whether he brought any money back from that night of card playing. But I had begun to see him in a new light.

Despite the way Dad squandered some of his earnings, Mother managed to put three meals on the table each day, though supper might be only fried potatoes seasoned with specks of bacon, or baked beans with bread she had made. My scrawniness was in no danger of being swaddled in fat.

My father had gone through rough times of his own. I offer that not to excuse his behavior but to complete the record. After he had completed his mandatory eight years of schooling in Java, he desperately wanted to attend high school.

"He wanted to play high school sports, especially basketball," Aunt Rose told me. It's not surprising that sport, rather than study, lured him at that age. He was a good athlete. But high school was out of the question. His family lived on a farm, and his father barred the way to high school, arguing that no one needed more than eight years of schooling. In truth, what his sons needed concerned him not at all. He wanted his sons to work for him. What else had he raised them for? Neither of my father's older brothers, Jake and John, had been permitted to attend high school, nor was his next younger brother, Fred. The girls in the family, Barbara, Katherine, Rose, and Frieda, not needed in the fields, were free to attend high school, but only the youngest boy, Carl, the baby of the family, was granted that privilege. By the time he reached high school age, the family had moved from farm to town, so his labor wasn't needed. When he graduated from high school, unable to find other satisfactory work, Carl enlisted in the Army. After his discharge, he attended the University of Minnesota and pitched for the university baseball team until he graduated. He later pitched for the Minneapolis Millers, rooming with teammate Ted Williams. A sore shoulder ended his baseball career shortly after he joined the Brooklyn Dodgers. He was called back into the Army during World War II and made a career of it. For Uncle Carl, if not for his brothers, high school was opportunity knocking.

Dad would have thrived in high school. He was quick-witted, adept with numbers and quick to calculate mathematical problems in his head, a fast talker when excited, a solid worker. He would have breezed through his courses while happily devoting himself to sports.

"Before he began boozing," Berthold (Snip) Schnaible, a contemporary of his once told me, "your dad was the best pitcher in the area, better than any of the guys we have today." I took his word for it. Snip Schnaible had spent years behind the plate, had caught the area's best pitchers.

I have a photograph of the Java baseball team, taken in the summer of 1923, a brick wall of the new Java school serving as backdrop. Six of my father's teammates, and the manager, squat or sprawl on the ground. Behind them stand five more players, Dad in the center, square-jawed and confident, a J on his uniform. He was twenty then. Snip Schnaible explained that the photograph had been taken after Java had played Mobridge, a larger town some thirty miles to the west.

"Java beat Mobridge," he said, "thanks to your dad. He won the game with a home run in a late inning."

By the time I heard this Dad was dead. He never told me he had played for the Java team.

Java baseball team, 1923

Of Dad's sisters, Barbara and Rose were each advanced two grades while in school, and each graduated as valedictorian of her class.

"I felt cheated having only ten years of school," Aunt Rose said. "I loved school." She had just turned seventeen when she graduated from high school in 1927. Her classmates included my mother and one of her sisters, Katherine. Rose enrolled in a college in Aberdeen in the fall, her goal being to teach English literature. Two months after she matriculated, in October, 1927, her mother died. Rose gave up her classes and came home to run the household. She never returned to college.

The family's other valedictorian, Barbara, four years older than Rose, had attended college for a year and earned a certificate that enabled her to teach in country schools. She married a farmer, Hank Lutz, and produced a bright and beautiful daughter, Elaine, born just two weeks after my own birth. She and I played together during family gatherings. I liked her cuteness, her quick mind, a girl seemingly headed for a bright future.

In the spring of 1940, Elaine accompanied her parents on a trip to Fort Yates, North Dakota, to visit her Aunt Rose, Uncle Gerhart, and cousin Delbert. Elaine and Aunt Rose were very close. As the visitors were about to leave, Elaine clung to her aunt.

"Come with us, Aunt Rose. Come stay with us for a while."

"Honey, I can't. You know we're coming down to see you next Sunday."

"You won't see me then."

"Sure I will. We'll play together."

"I won't be there."

When telling me the story, Rose said that Elaine had spoken earnestly, clinging to her and begging her to accompany them, insisting that Rose wouldn't see her on Sunday.

Children often say nonsensical things. You won't see me. I won't be there. Any number of seemingly outlandish statements. And most such utterances are quickly forgotten. Only when they become prophetic are they remembered.

On the following Thursday afternoon, after riding the school bus home and having a snack, Elaine went outside to play with her dog while her parents began milking their cows. Moments later Barbara called for her daughter. No answer. Suddenly alarmed, Barb and Hank began a frantic search. Coming to the creek that ran through their property, they spotted the tip of Elaine's hair ribbon floating on the water, her body upright beneath the surface. Hank jumped in and pulled his daughter from five feet of water, rushed her to the nearest town, Selby, but resuscitation efforts failed. My brilliant cousin with the bright future had drowned at age eight.

Children fantasize, write fanciful stories. Unless a mother is a sentimental collector, the stories often are discarded and forgotten, along with the fantasies.

Barbara later found among Elaine's school work a story she had written, a story about a girl who slipped into deep water and was rescued by her dog. One can imagine links here, one can imagine possibilities, but one can never know how Elaine came to be submerged in that creek. What she said to her aunt, and the girlish story she wrote, aren't completely compatible. They could have been mere coincidence. But, as Aunt Rose said, "One wonders."

We traveled to Java for the services, first a solemn family wake at the home of my Goetz grandparents. Uncle Gerhart led his son Delbert and me to Elaine's open casket on its stand in my grandparents' living room. Bouquets of commercial flowers rimmed the casket, their scent different from the flowers I knew.

"See how peacefully she's sleeping," Uncle Gerhart said, cupping his palm against her cheek. He said it to help us through her death, but he knew that we knew better. She looked peaceful, her eyelids delicately closed, her girlish cheeks and mouth pleasantly composed, no sign of her agonal struggle beneath the water. She looked as if she might be asleep, but I knew better. She's dead, I thought, overcome by sadness. She's dead. And surrounded by flowers.

Since then I've seen only one other who looked as peaceful and beautiful as Elaine in death. For a short time while serving as a medical intern, I covered a small satellite of a large county hospital and was on duty one afternoon when an ambulance brought a young woman in. The attendants didn't rush her in. They knew haste was useless. I was called as a formality, to pronounce her dead. She lay on a gurney as if she were sleeping, her forehead smooth, her eyes closed, her attractive face serene. A sheet covered her from the neck down. I pulled the sheet back to expose her naked chest and listened with my stethoscope to the silence of her lungs and heart. I drew the sheet further down to reveal her abdomen. There, an inch to the left of her umbilicus, pouted a small red circle, the entry wound for a bullet I was told had been fired by her estranged husband. I pulled the sheet back up to her neck and glanced again at her composed features, which gave no sign of her agonal struggle as blood had gushed from the punctured aorta into her abdomen and drained her life. She appeared to be a gorgeous sleeping brunette, ready to reawaken to a full life. But sadly she was dead. And lying on a gurney.

After our morning wake for Elaine, we moved on to the Lutheran church, where her casket and accompanying flowers brightened the altar already crowded with commercial bouquets. I disliked their heavy fragrance, which was so unlike that of wild flowers I knew, and unlike that of flowers grown by my grandmother in her garden. Aunt Barbara wept uncontrollably for her daughter, Aunt Rose for her niece. When the service ended and casket was closed for the final time, Barbara and Rose clutched the ornate box, unwilling to let go. I breathed the heavy air, my eyes wet. For years afterward, I hated the scent of florists's flowers.

Once, while we were reminiscing over the telephone, Aunt Rose described a side of my father I never knew.

"Your dad laughed a lot when he was young," Rose said. "He loved to kid around, and he was always kind to us girls. He was protective of our mother, too. And that got him into big trouble. Our dad was mean to us kids, mean to our mother too. Isn't that a terrible thing to say about your own father? Once he was so furious that he threw our shoemaker's last at Mother. It missed and broke when it hit the floor. George grabbed our dad from behind and pinned him, wouldn't let go until the old fool cooled down, at least toward our mother. But he turned all his bile on George and told him to get out of the house and never come back. George was about seventeen then. It was winter, very cold that day."

Rose abruptly stopped, as if she had come to the end of the story. I waited through a long silence.

"Very cold?" I said at last.

"I don't know how your dad found a place to stay," she said, "don't know where he went. He had no money. He had to walk to town in the cold. It happened early on a Saturday. I was about ten at the time, and we kids went to Saturday school at the church. When we drove to town later that day, I worried about George. I chewed my nails until every finger bled. Carl and I talked about it afterward. He said the old man had walked around our farm yard that afternoon with a shotgun, to scare George off if he tried to return. I've often wondered whether that day caused some of your dad's later problems."

I was willing to believe it, wanted to believe it. Rejected, not a dollar to his name, Dad needed to find shelter, food to sustain him. As he slogged from the family farm toward Java in that biting winter cold, did he sense a devilish tempter tiptoeing into his empty pockets? How many hours or days did it take for him to discover that a couple of stiff drinks straight from the bottle blurred worry over his poverty and wondrously eased his misery?

If George was seventeen when he was banished from the family home, it probably happened in the winter of 1919. Of what he did for the next fifteen years I know very little. Among other work, he hired out to work with farmers. He stayed in or near Java except when he worked on the Fort Peck dam in Montana, and when he enlisted in the Merchant Marine. I know nothing about his time in the service, other than he boxed for his unit. Rose thinks he enlisted in 1923 or 1924. After his discharge his father forgave him at last and welcomed him back into his home in town. The family had given up farming in 1926 and bought a house in Java.

"George was still a prankster when he came out of the Merchant Marine," Aunt Rose said. "Always joking and laughing."

Dad had toned down his laughing by the time I knew him, but he and I got along well in Onida. I began to recognize his moods, his tendencies. I could predict what he would say in certain circumstances. When someone talked nonsense and tried to get Dad to agree, saying something like, "It's so simple, George, can't you see that?" Dad would respond, "I see, said the blind man, as he picked up the hammer and saw." This comment often zipped right over the head of the nincompoop. And when someone told

Dad of a fatal car crash and blamed it on speeding, Dad invariably would say, "It's not the speed that kills you; it's the sudden stop."

He tried to make a ball player out of me. He bought me a small baseball glove, a ball and bat. We played catch or pitched while the other batted. If I clubbed the ball some twenty-five yards to our sidewalk, I considered it a monster hit.

"How far can you hit it?" I asked.

"To the other side of the street."

"To that house?" I pointed to the one to the east.

"Yes."

It seemed impossible. "Do it," I said. "Smash it as far as you can." I wanted to be impressed, to be proud of him. He refused. In my disappointment I thought he had exaggerated. I doubted he could hit a ball that far.

Years later I revisited that spot in Onida and saw that a man who could hit home runs could easily drive a baseball much farther than Dad had indicated, could drive it well beyond the house across the street. And I saw the large and inviting the windows of that house, windows expensive for a man to replace when he's earning forty dollars a month.

I contracted my share of childhood diseases in Onida: chicken pox, both kinds of measles, even scarlet fever. Mumps caught up with me a few years later. Placards, red as I recall, were nailed outside our doors to warn others that our house was quarantined, a futile effort to prevent the spread of contagions. When I came down with scarlet fever, the precautions were strict. Mother submerged our empty milk bottles in a pan of boiling water and set it outside for the milkman, who retrieved the bottles from the cooled water when he delivered fresh milk. But my illnesses weren't severe. I passed through each without difficulty.

When Mother was young, as I've mentioned, she too contracted scarlet fever. But she wasn't as lucky as I. Her attack evolved into a more serious illness, acute glomerulonephritis, a disorder characterized by inflammation of glomeruli in the kidneys. The glomeruli, those extraordinary tufts of permeable capillaries, filter clear liquid from blood and channel it into renal tubules, thus beginning the process of urine formation. Mother's glomerulonephritis festered chronically. Her first signs of renal impairment appeared during her initial pregnancy, when she carried me.

My young eyes saw no evidence of her illness. She was unstoppable while we were in Onida, a ceaseless force preparing meals, frying potatoes on the kerosine stove, baking meat loaf and casseroles in its oven, baking breads, making dumplings. Her hands were pistons when she scrubbed our clothes on her washboard. She rinsed them by hand and hung them outside on a line to dry. She ironed practically everything, including our underwear, pressing each piece with her old-fashioned iron, its inserts heated on a metal plate on the stove. When one insert cooled, she exchanged it for a hot one on the stove, snapping the heated one into the iron's handle. The inserts fit loosely in the handle and clicked each time she changed directions on the cloth. On countless mornings I awoke to the click of her iron, unaware of her festering disease, knowing only that she liked to get an early start on the day.

She prepared herself for her cleaning chores by putting her hair up and wrapping a large red, white, and blue kerchief neatly around her head, tying it in front with a neat small knot, the stubby ends poking out like a miniature bow tie. Seeing Mother prepare for her chores through the distance that now separates us, I wonder. Did she, as she tied her neat bow, recognize how desperately she was striving to keep the fraying ends of her life together? Did she see better days ahead - or only darkness? With her head brightly dressed for action, she blazed through the house, sweeping and scrubbing floors, dusting, attacking grime wherever she found it. She had been reared to believe that cleanliness was next to Godliness, and she paid homage to both. "It's good," she often told me, "to keep the house spick-and-span." And she did.

But her glomerulonephritis was stealthily sapping her energy even as she pretended to be fine. In the spring of 1940, her younger sister, Ella, married in Java. Mother could have taken a bus and attended the wedding, a trip of less than two hours. But Aunt Ella recalls that Mother, who at the time was six months into her third pregnancy, wrote and apologized for being unable to attend the wedding. She would love to come, she wrote, but she was too sick to travel. I knew nothing of that letter.

Mother, perhaps concerned about my social development, especially my interaction with girls, passed along hints from time to time. She took special care to ground me in the intricacies of May Day baskets, telling me that I should fill small baskets with flowers and candy and place them on the doorsteps of girls I particularly admired. And, she added with a mischievous smile, I was duty bound to kiss any girl who saw me deliver a basket and chased and caught me. At her prompting, I cut a couple of baskets from colored paper and filled them with dandelions and peppermint candy. I pretended I did it only to please her, but the prospect of being caught and kissed carried an appeal that seemed deliciously wicked. I delivered the baskets, rapped once at each door, and tore away. The girls gave chase but had little chance to catch me. I foolishly barreled away at full tilt.

A few baskets ended up on my doorstep. Mother saw one approaching.

"I think you're getting a May basket."

Someone knocked. I flew to the back door, glanced at the basket on the stoop and saw Delores, one of my classmates, dashing up the street. I gave chase and nabbed her before she'd gone a block. Facing her, with her lips inches from mine, I hesitated, suddenly uncomfortable. But I thought of Mother's coaching, remembered the process. That got me though it. I leaned closer and kissed Delores soundly on the lips. She, the first girl I ever kissed, robustly kissed me back.

I don't think sex education was taught in Dakota elementary schools in my day; it certainly wasn't in the schools I attended. Sex was much less a public matter then, something kids learned about in the alleys. Though formal education would have been helpful, it would have been largely redundant. The basic information, admittedly garbled, readily trickled down to the youngest of students. While I was in the second grade in Onida, Owen and I found a pair of girls willing to broaden our education - and theirs. One girl was a classmate of ours, the other a year younger. We four slipped into a half-empty storage shed for an extended period of impromptu study. There, among a collection of rusting implements, securely away from prying adult eyes, Owen and I removed our shirts, then our jeans. The girls hesitantly pulled their dresses over their heads. Owen and I tossed off our shoes and socks, our underwear, coaxed the girls out of theirs. With not a stitch of clothing to impede us, we four explored with a bumbling but eager diligence, taking our drill quite seriously, tutoring and being tutored first by one, then the other, taking what we thought was full measure from the opportunity. Though perhaps each of us sensed that even more amazing enlightenments lay in our future, we were, I think, quite satisfied with the load of valuable new information we gathered in our sublime isolation.

The following day, as I passed through the alley that ran behind the younger girl's home, her mother rushed onto the porch and screamed at me.

"What did you do with my daughter yesterday?"

I was shocked by the outburst. It had not occurred to me that her daughter would kiss and tell, but the tone and volume of her mother's voice left no doubt that I had been betrayed. I immediately lost respect for the girl and her loose lips. Because her mother obviously had key pieces of information at hand, some highly incriminating even if she didn't have the full story, I saw no reason to linger and listen to her wrath. Nor was I eager to divulge any details her daughter might have overlooked. Keeping my eyes straight ahead, pretending not to hear, I quickened my steps, sensing the mother's eyes scorching my back and wondering whether she was giving chase. When I reached the home of our neighbors to the north, I cut through their yard and slipped into our house, nervously expecting a pounding on the door, expecting the indignant woman to burst in and scream to Mother that I had sullied her daughter. My nervousness, derived from culpability not remorse, was overblown. I heard no more of the matter.

The neighbors who owned the yard I escaped through, the Larsons, were congenial. They and my parents often stood out in the back yard talking after supper, laughing into the night. Mr. Larson managed the town's grain elevators and became duly impressed with Dad's industry, so much so that he hired him to help run the elevators. At first Dad worked part-time as his schedule allowed, supplementing his income from the WPA. Afterward he switched to full-time with Mr. Larson.

His persistent hard work and initiative so impressed his new boss that Mr. Larson recommended him for another job: manager of the grain elevator in Timber Lake. Dad interviewed for the job and was hired on the spot. Mother and I cheered the news. Dad was moving up in the world. We would rise as well. With that job beckoning, we packed our things and prepared to move to Timber Lake, South Dakota, late in the summer of 1940.

CHAPTER 4

We loaded everything we owned into an old borrowed truck for our move to Timber Lake, wedging quilts and blankets between the heavier pieces of furniture to minimize damage on the road. With the truck filled up above the side rails, we walked through our little house one last time, the space oddly smaller when empty. Our echoing footsteps made me sad. I wouldn't miss the house, but leaving my friends was another matter. Mother sensed my mood and put a hand on my shoulder.

"Look at the bright side," she said. "Dad has a better job. No more commodities for us."

I knew she was right, and I felt better when we came out into the sunshine. It was late summer, warm and windless, with a few baby clouds floating in the skim-milk sky, a fine day to travel to another part of the world. Though I judged Timber Lake to be incredibly far away, it lay only about a hundred and twenty miles to the northwest. In that pre-television era, much of what little I knew of the planet had come filtered through the movie screen.

I'd learned of our larger cities, knew of the unbelievably tall Empire State Building, had seen views of beautiful Washington, D.C., where President Roosevelt lived, but would have struggled to pinpoint any of these places on a map. I knew that most of my grandfather Schafer's relatives lived to the north, in Canada. And of course everyone in our second grade class knew that China was on the opposite side of the world from us, that if you dug a hole deep enough...

Just that summer I had heard of a man named Hitler whose armies were smashing through countries on a continent called Europe. In the darkness of the Onida theater I had watched newsreels showing German heavy guns belch dark fumes, jerking each time they fired. I had seen helmeted troops running through mud, throwing themselves down flat and picking off unseen targets with their rifles. Only weeks before we packed to move, I'd watched troops goose-stepping smartly along a boulevard in a French town called Paris. Such images inspired us boys to play war games and send each other to a thousand deaths. We pretended we had rifles, that armies backed us with tanks and heavy artillery, but in the end we settled each battle with primitive combat, our favorite weapon being spears, dried sunflower stalks barbed with dirt-clumped roots. The armies that inspired us, those flickering on the Onida screen, were as distant as the moon, and caused us no worry at all.

In the bright sunshine, Dad gave our load its final inspection. When Mother, Carol in her arms, headed for the cab, I impulsively volunteered to ride in back, telling Dad I'd monitor the load and watch for shifts that might scratch or break something. Not that I expected any shifting. I thought it would be neat to ride perched atop the load with the open air blowing over me. It would be the perfect spot from which to watch the passing landscape as we neared Timber Lake, which is located "west river," that is west of the Missouri. Dad, in an effort to lower my resistance to the move, had painted a glowing picture of the west-river topography, its impressive buttes and broad rolling hills.

When the truck backed onto the street, its rusted muffler roaring and belching a nasty metallic exhaust that burned my eyes, I perched gingerly on a cardboard box packed with clothing. I managed to stay reasonably upright until we rattled over the railroad tracks. A sudden lurch tipped me onto the sharp edge of a small table, scratching my arm and sending a warning. When we got up to speed on the highway, the cargo came alive, jiggling and shifting with every dip and bulge in the road, throwing me about. I anxiously crawled from place to place, trying to find a stable spot where I could ride in peace. I longed to be up front but didn't want to be a sissy and ask Dad to stop.

The only good part of the trip came when we slipped across the Missouri. Thanks to the smooth roadway on the bridge, the truck glided over it with minimal jiggle. I got a good look at the river, which I'd never seen before. At first I judged it to be a wide boring stream, sluggish and dotted with sandbars. Then I spotted the swirls and eddies, the rush of muddy water, small trees and branches sweeping along in the current. The river was narrower then, more rugged, not yet tamed and broadened by the Oahe Dam which would convert that stretch of the Old Muddy into broad and deep Lake Oahe. Once we passed over the bridge, the jolting and thumping resumed. I toughed it out until the truck hit a pot hole that rattled the cargo like an earthquake and tumbled me into a gap between a dresser and a table. I'd had enough. I struggled free and crawled up and banged on the rear window of the cab.

Dad grinned when he pulled over to stop. I climbed into the cab with great relief and settled between him and Mother, who held Carol on her pregnancy-diminished lap. I'd been so concerned about my safety in back that I hadn't noticed the changing landscape, the scattered buttes, nor had I noticed the sky had clouded over.

"There it is," Dad said.

In the distance Timber Lake's water tower and grain elevator broke above the horizon. The grain elevator was covered with iron siding, corrugated and galvanized to the same grayness as the elevators in Onida, so it presented a familiar and comforting appearance. But this elevator turned out to be different. It had living quarters attached to the elevator's office, a few small rooms that were to house us. I don't remember the rooms well enough to describe them, other than to say they were dark and depressing, and that our living room connected through a doorway to the elevator's office. The layout of the rest of the rooms is inexplicably lost. For some reason, many of my Timber Lake experiences have faded from view and become as imperceptible as catfish swimming along the bottom of a murky creek.

As always, I automatically oriented myself to my surroundings upon arrival and noted among other things that the railroad tracks beside the elevator ran north and south. When I stepped outside early the next morning, something was out of kilter. My surroundings were askew. After uncomfortable floundering, I identified the problem. The sun had been knocked off its course. It was rising directly over the railroad tracks to the south. I, always so right with the world, wanted to fault the sun, but the truth was self-evident. Somehow, while bouncing around in back of the truck, I had lost my orientation and had entered Timber Lake ninety degrees out of phase. It was a perception solidly ingrained. For the two years we lived in Timber Lake, my sun stubbornly rose in the south and set in the north.

School began within days of our arrival. Though a twitter of nervousness ran through me on the morning I was to enroll in the third grade, again knowing no one, I felt reasonably confident. I'd seen how the school system worked in Onida and expected few differences here. The towns were roughly equal in size. And I had another important reason for confidence. Dad had a real job now. We had moved beyond the WPA and commodities.

My third grade class shared a common room with the fourth grade students in a new school building, its poured-concrete exterior pleasingly modern, its classrooms sparkling with shiny hardwood floors, its interior smelling of new wood and varnish. Our teacher, Miss Pearson, divided her time between our two classes, a system I liked. Though we third-graders received only half of Miss Pearson's attention, I didn't mind. I listened as she taught fourth grade subjects. Through this tidy arrangement, I learned short division and long division simultaneously.

I recently came across a group photograph, a bit mangled, of those who shared our room that year. Thirteen girls sit in the front row, legs demurely crossed at their ankles, hands folded. Though most of the faces are familiar, I can recall the full names of but two. Behind the girls stand seventeen boys, and Miss Pearson. I can name only five of the boys, one being me. The lad I once was stands clear-eyed and - perhaps I only imagine it from this distance - vulnerable. Seeing the future he does not, I feel a sudden urge to whisper a word of encouragement across the gulf that separates us, to fortify him for what lies ahead.

While in Onida, I had taken careful note of the distinct pecking order of school boys, an order that bore an imperfect relationship to physical strength. Attitude appeared more important than muscles. As an unknown newcomer, I was determined to take my place near the top of any existing order, though I was of no more than average strength. During one of our first recesses, I wandered around the playground looking for a candidate to make my statement to. The one I chose wore gray coveralls, stood perhaps an inch taller than I, and appeared to be fairly sturdy.

"Bet I can take you down," I said, fashioning a facial expression intended to convey my most positive attitude.

"Bet you can't."

We squared off and circled uncertainly between the teeter-totters and the swings until we drew a crowd. I tinkered with a scowl, tried to look invincible. When we finally threw ourselves at each other, our onlookers predictably aligned themselves against the new kid in town and screamed for his blood. Our skirmish was short. I realized it was over when my view of the Timber Lake sky refused to change, a view partially obscured by the head of my opponent. It wasn't the crowd's will that landed me on my back. I unknowingly had challenged the strongest boy in my class, a boy with a fine positive attitude of his own. My blunder didn't matter. I soon had a cluster of new friends.

It was a time when nearly all men smoked. My Onida friends and I had taken our share of puffs on pilfered cigarettes, or on discarded butts picked off the street, in anticipation of our coming manhood. We Timber Lake boys were similarly inclined. Someone invented ersatz cigarettes and spread the word. Dozens of dull pencils began to assault the pencil sharpener before recess, filling it with shavings. One of us emptied the sharpener into the waste basket and diverted most of the refuse onto a sheet of paper that was folded carefully and slipped into a pocket. During recess we conspirators headed for the edge of the school yard and hunkered down into a shallow ditch where, with tablet paper and shredded pencils, we rolled our own and lit them with wooden matches, drew in the distasteful smoke and pretended it was rich, fresh tobacco, nodding sagely but avoiding each other's eyes.

After a few puffs I looked to the school yard for help, hoping a teacher would see our smoke and rescue us. No luck. We turned glassy-eyed as the offensive residue of burning wood and carbon curled around us, slowly doing us in. We went back to scrounging butts off the sidewalk.

Within a month of our arrival, Mother gave birth. The October 3rd, 1940, *Java Herald* announced the arrival of Betty Jane, her third child. *Born to Mr. and Mrs. George Goetz of Timber Lake, on Friday, September 27, a fine baby girl. Congratulations! Grandpa and Grandma, Mr. and Mrs. Jacob Schafer, went to Timber Lake Friday to meet the new granddaughter and Mrs. Schafer remained to be with her daughter for a few weeks.*

Births, like deaths, draw relatives. Aunt Rose and her son, Delbert, and her sister, Barbara, drove down from Fort Yates one Sunday morning to see the sparkling new baby. Coming to Timber Lake to visit her brother and his family must have been difficult for Barbara, her daughter Elaine's drowning still fresh in her mind. Elaine and I, born two weeks and a few miles apart, had learned to crawl, to walk, to talk, almost simultaneously. Now I was a lively eight-year old and Barbara's daughter lay still in her hill-top grave in the Java cemetery. And her brother and sister-in-law had a new baby daughter.

Aunt Rose, speaking with me by telephone when she was eighty-seven, remembered their trip to Timber Lake with sparkling clarity. "The fall colors were unusually beautiful that year," she said. "I don't think I've ever seen trees more colorful."

"Betty rarely cried," Rose continued. "And her older sister was shy. Carol would close her eyes and think we couldn't see her." My aunt bubbled on, happily remembering details of her visit a half century earlier as clearly as if they had happened the week before. Her memory shamed me. I couldn't even recall their visit.

I once helped Dad empty grain from one of the elevator's bins. We waded through a huge sloping pile of wheat, sunk to our knees in tons of golden-tan kernels that flowed smoothly into a slot in the floor. From there a chain-driven hoist lifted the grain and diverted it into a railroad boxcar. Most of the work was done by gravity, the wheat sliding down its slope like sand slipping through an hour glass. We speeded up the process with our scoop shovels, raising a fine dust.

"You want to take over?" Dad asked, abruptly stopping his work. "I need to leave for a minute."

Sure I did. It was easy work. I assumed he was headed for the privy.

"Keep the wheat feeding into the slot," he said when leaving me in charge. "Don't let the mechanism run dry."

I oozed through the wheat, occasionally assisting gravity with my scoop shovel, circling from one part of the slope to another, the weight of sliding wheat pressing pleasantly on my legs, the dry dust tickling my throat. Time passed, the slope decreased, the wheat slid more slowly, I began to use my shovel more often. Then gravity and I were doing equal work, and I, seeing what was coming, waited anxiously for assistance. What was Dad doing? Pushing the wheat with more effort, I began to sweat. Soon the only grain entering the slot was that scooped by me. And each scoopful I threw into it, like chaff in a gale, flew instantly away. My muscles ached, my back hurt, and I, fearing the mechanism would run dry, shoveled harder. If it ran dry and broke, Dad might have to pay for the repair. I couldn't stop to rest. Gasping for breath, coughing and gagging, my lungs clogged with grain dust, I shoveled on, unable to go for help because the mechanism would run completely empty. That surely would ruin it. I was trapped. I was tired. Where was he? Exhausted, fearing I would collapse any moment, I threw wheat at the slot, seething with anger. After an eternity, Dad returned.

"Where were you?" I screamed. "I couldn't keep up."

"A customer came in. It's okay. Nothing would have broken." He picked up his shovel and casually attacked the last of the wheat.

That was it? Nothing would have broken? What was he talking about? Hadn't he told me not to let the mechanism run dry? What was that supposed to mean? I was furious with him, with his lack of concern, with his damnable calm manner. Didn't he know what he had put me through? It was this I wanted him to admit, that he had set me up. I wanted him to recognize that I had given the task everything I had. When he didn't, I threw my shovel down and stalked out.

About this time Mother became seriously ill. It strikes me as odd that I remember so clearly my skirmish with the wheat but remember her attack not at all. Aunt Ella refreshed my memory. She was newly married then and living on a farm south of Java.

"Your dad drove over from Timber Lake late one evening in the spring of 1941," Ella told me. "I think it was in April, saying Emma was sick in bed, too weak to care for you kids, too weak to cook or clean, too weak to stand up."

We didn't have a car at the time, so Dad must have borrowed one.

"He asked if I could come over and help out, and I did. You don't remember my being there? You still lived in the elevator then."

How could I have forgotten? Stress surely was high when Mother went down, unable to leave her bed. Carol was three, Betty an infant. I suppose Dad and I did what we could before he went for help.

"How long were you with us?" I asked.

"About two weeks. I cleaned and cooked and took care of Emma. She wasn't able to get out of bed until the day before I left. The folks and Ted came to get me."

The folks were her parents, my Schafer grandparents, and Ted was Ted Buechler, Ella's first husband. Bothered that I remembered none of this, I used Ella's account as a probe and struggled to tap into that distant black hole. I failed. The powerful dark gravity of that distant turmoil allowed not a single image of my bedridden mother to escape.

A feed store, an adjunct to the elevator's business and managed by my father, launched its operation in the summer of 1941. This development enabled us to leave the elevator's stifling quarters for slightly better ones. The feed store occupied the right half of a single-story building on Timber Lake's Main Street. The left side contained a set of three small rooms which became our new home. In front was the living room that could be entered either through the front door from the sidewalk on Main Street, or from an interior door connecting directly with the feed store. Behind the living room was a small bedroom, and beyond that the kitchen, primitive and tiny. The bedroom had no doors, merely archways that provided access to the kitchen and living room.

The beds of my parents and sisters filled the little sleeping chamber. I spent my nights on the fold-down couch in the living room. The living room had special appeal because my parents, in a sudden splurge, had bought a radio and installed it on a shelf opposite the couch, its power provided through an extension cord that looped outward from the center of the ceiling, connected to the room's only electrical outlet. Through that radio I heard President Roosevelt's address after the Japanese bombing of Pearl Harbor late in 1941. It was a mild December day in that part of

South Dakota. Our front door was open, and I stood on the sidewalk outside, listening to our president's powerful voice boom through the screen door as he described the "day of infamy." His words stirred me. I thought of the war scenes I'd seen on film, the war games I'd played, with growing excitement. We were going to war. But our president didn't sound thrilled. He sounded angry and troubled. And my parents didn't sound at all thrilled. They were upset with the Japanese and, as far as I could tell, upset with Roosevelt as well.

Betty was walking by the time we entered the war. She and Carol often played in the space behind our kitchen, a hard-packed patch of ground that separated our back door from the structure that housed ovens of the town's bakery. The ovens gave off wonderful aromas. The baker and his assistants passed through our back yard several times daily, carrying trays of warm sweet rolls and breads from the ovens to the retail bakery, located next door to the feed store on Main Street. Carol and Betty now and then snared free samples from the kindly baker, usually jelly-filled doughnuts, and shared them with me.

One time on an errand to the bakery, I overheard a customer joshing with the baker.

"Louie, the mayor tells me he's going to have to close you down, put you out of business."

"Why's that?" the baker asked, handing me my loaf.

"He says too many women are getting bread here."

The baker chuckled. From their manner I gathered that the men assumed the little witticism had flown straight over my young head. Not wishing to set them straight, I locked my expression in neutral until I reached the sidewalk. I was young enough to consider the word play quite inventive and later raised a chorus of chuckles while passing the joke around to my buddies.

Our living room radio came to an unfortunate end. Timber Lake holds an annual summer celebration, the Days of 1910, which was supplemented by a traveling carnival that set up rides and other attractions. Our parents surprised me one evening by proclaiming they were going dancing and had hired a sitter to care for Carol, Betty, and me. They were, they said proudly, taking an evening out. Having a sitter was a first, and I acted up, showing off for the girl watching over us, pretending that I too was at the dance. I invited a broom to be my partner and spun through the living room, quite gracefully I thought, until the broom's handle hooked the drooping electrical cord and jerked the radio from its shelf.

Even at that age guilt settled easily on me. It shot through me while the radio was still in flight and lodged heavily in my gut as our prized source of entertainment scattered itself in pieces across the floor. With my earlier cockiness so abruptly blown away, I raged at myself for being so stupid and brooded compulsively until my parents returned after midnight. I expected the worst, knew I deserved whatever punishment would come my way. I was shocked by their leniency - and relieved. I was given no penalty, other than a couple of months without radio entertainment, a deprivation suffered by all of us, innocent and guilty alike, until money had accumulated to fund a replacement.

One evening during the summer festival three of us boys walked along the brightly-lit row of tents and booths to check out the carnival's attractions. A good crowd was on hand. A small calliope blared. Somewhere delicious hamburgers fried. Men lined up to throw baseballs at rows of flat rag dolls fitted with fringes to make them look wider than they were.

"Knock three down and win a prize," the man behind the counter said. Most of the baseballs flew between the dolls or over their heads.

As the baseballs whizzed past the dolls and thumped into the back of the tent, an amplified voice rose above the noise, saying something like "huzza, huzza, huzza." Turning around, I saw a bald man dressed in a brilliant white shirt and bow tie standing on a small platform directly across from us. He held a microphone close to his mouth.

"Good evening, ladies and gentlemen," he said. "Step closer, please."

As my buddies and I obeyed, the man lapsed into a string of meaningless sounds. It may have been a foreign language. More likely it was mumbo-jumbo. People passing by paused to see what he was up to.

"All right, ladies and gentlemen," he said after a crowd had gathered. "Here's what you've been waiting for. Take a look at this." On cue, a scantily-clad woman emerged from the tent behind him and pranced onto the platform. She wore a silky gown parted in front to reveal a black gauzy under layer. Through the dark gauze I could see outlines of her black brassiere and black panties. My friends and I moved in close to watch the woman wiggle and sway her hips provocatively while the barker hinted at the marvelously interesting sights to be revealed inside the tent behind him. The man's spiel intensified, hooking my buddies and me. We had to get into that tent. And, with surprisingly little difficulty, we did, crouching low and shuffling along unseen in the throng entering with tickets.

A low wooden platform, no more than six inches off the ground, had been roped off at the back end of the tent. On this makeshift stage stood a phonograph and a small wooden box. The rest of the tent provided standing room only. As we boys fought our way toward the stage, I felt a blend of embarrassment and guilt, not knowing exactly what to expect but certain that the woman would reveal more of herself than she had outside the tent. I had a strong suspicion that I was stepping into a filthy gutter, but the pull of adventure out-muscled guilt and embarrassment.

We three aggressively wriggled our way forward to the stage, ending up front and center with the rope pressing tightly against our chests. No one seemed to object to the presence of a few nine-year-old kids. Behind us a crowd of men, and a few women, had poured into the tent until its sidewalls bulged. The air was heavy with cigarette smoke, penetrating masculine sweat, and second-hand alcohol. I felt a thrill of anticipation, and wondered guiltily what Mother would think if she could see me now.

Our performer stepped onto the low stage and sent a couple of saucy winks our way. She began to limber up and exchange patter with men in the audience. Her warmup was similar to that of an athlete stretching before competition but modified to give peculiar emphasis to the parts of her anatomy that distinguished her as a woman. Her suggestive stretching intensified, sending surges of energy our way. Though I had little experience judging a woman's age, I estimated she was in her mid-thirties, She was generously built but not fat, her pleasant facial features edged with that easily-recognizable but difficult-to-describe expression that proclaims: *I've had a rough life, buster, don't mess with me.* I concluded that she, as I'd heard adults say of certain women, had been around the block a time or two.

When the center of our attention was satisfied that she, not to mention her audience, was sufficiently warmed up, she put a record on her wind-up phonograph, peeled off her silky robe, and began to shimmy around the platform, keeping time with the scratchy music. How much would she take off? All of it, I hoped, my guilt suddenly absent in the heat of her performance. Our entertainer showed herself to be an efficient, if not notably graceful, stripper, throwing off her gauzy nighty with a leer, strutting more vigorously before unsnapping her brassiere and sliding it slowly down her arms to reveal the sizeable masses it had concealed, each one tipped with a tiny sparkling cone. And, last of all and with much fanfare, she began to roll down the top of her skimpy black panties inch by inch, gyrating furiously all the while, to reveal her natural shield. Golly. Then, with no hint of embarrassment, she pushed that garment down to her knees, stepped out of it, and tossed it over her shoulder. I could hardly believe it. There she stood, completely naked but for two inconsequential cones, her womanhood exposed, directly across the rope from me. I joined in the enthusiastic applause, wickedly thrilled by her brief performance, and waited for the crowd to sift out of the tent. But no one moved. Would there be more?

As if to answer my silent question, the performer sashayed over to the wooden box beside her phonograph and, carefully directing her backside toward us, casually bent over to collect a few things from the box. Oh my God. Would she actually use those? The main show, I understood, was about to begin.

Her performance was, in a word, raunchy. Making adroit use of her various props, spicing her varied muscular strainings with descriptive comments, crude and direct, our star of the evening threw her feeble light into the darkest of alleys. I was repelled. I was fascinated. I did not bat an eye.

"It's not real, honey," she said at one point, undergoing certain contortions while making one of her props slowly disappear. "But I wish it was."

The comments from men behind us were equally vulgar, though I paid little attention to them. I scrutinized the lewd performance from beginning to end, applauding with others each astonishing new development, even the minor early eye opener when she peeled off her tiny cones. We three youngsters stood our ground wide-eyed, taking note of every jiggle, every muscle twitch, gaping, at times involuntarily gasping, at the extraordinary level of entertainment available to us in our little town of Timber Lake.

Our family had never owned a car, nothing other than the Model A pickup truck on the ranch, which may or may not have been ours, and had disappeared after we left the ranch. Thus it was a great surprise one day when my father parked a green 1935 Chevrolet sedan in front of our place on Main Street. We saw him through the window.

"Who's car is that?" Mother asked.

"It's ours," I shouted, wishing out loud. "Dad bought it." I was half right. It was ours, but he hadn't bought it. He had won it in a poker game. We had the car for less than a year - until Dad's fortunes at the poker table turned.

As part of his job, Dad also was in charge of the grain elevator in Firesteel, a tiny town ten miles to the west, which he manned on certain days. He would travel there periodically, perhaps once a week, to open the Firesteel elevator for business. Memory fails to explain how he got to Firesteel before he acquired the Chevy. Maybe he hopped a freight, or took the bus, or caught a ride with someone. After he won the Chevy, I drove with him to Firesteel once and wandered about to inspect the facilities while he attended to his customers, weighing their trucks loaded with wheat, oats, or corn, assaying the grain for moisture and contaminants and docking the price accordingly, then weighing the empty trucks after they had dumped their cargo down the chute.

After he finished his duties for the day, we drove down to the local tavern and joined a row of men sitting on stools along the bar. Dad ordered a schooner of beer for himself and, knowing I had a taste for the brew, a short one for me. His cost ten cents;

mine, a nickel. Through a haze of cigarette smoke I watched in disbelief as the bartender drew up my draft. Cool glass in hand, pretending to be a man, I slouched against the bar and pressed my mouth through foam and drank. It was a delicious experience. Dad bantered with the other men, occasionally drawing me into the discussion. I perched happily on my bar stool, taking in every word. By watching carefully I timed my final tip of the glass to coincide with my father's, then wiped my mouth with the back of my wrist. In today's society, perhaps even in the tiny village of Firesteel, one could get into serious trouble for serving beer to a young boy. For the record, I wasn't corrupted by those few swallows of beer. On the contrary, that nickel's worth of lager was one of the finest investments my father ever made. That distant afternoon still vibrates in memory: a bright interval drawing son and father firmly together, as close as we would ever be.

On our way back to Timber Lake, Dad pulled onto the shoulder of the graveled highway and stopped.

"What's wrong?" I said.

"It's time you learned to drive," he said. He opened his door and came around to my side, leaving the engine running. Thrilled, I slipped behind the steering wheel and received my instructions: push in the clutch and move the long, curved floor shift lever into low gear. I tried to follow his instructions while craning my neck to see over the obstructing dashboard and hood - and stalled the car. He patiently had me try again. With a lurch I got the tires rolling over the loose gravel, but when it came time to shift into second gear, there was too much to consider at once, continue steering, push in the clutch, move the gear shift up, over, and up some more, let out the clutch. I attempted it, ended up in neutral, and had to start over in low gear. Another lurch. Another abrupt stop.

"Let's work together," Dad said. "When you push in the clutch, I'll shift into second for you."

It worked. After I'd picked up a bit of speed, Dad dropped it into third as my foot pushed down against the left pedal. It was impossible to keep the car going straight. I overcompensated for every deviation. Driving, I discovered, was far more complicated than simply steering a slow-moving pickup over prairie grass.

"Don't turn the wheel so far," Dad advised. We swayed along the road.

Though I drove scant minutes on that lonely road and covered no more than a few miles, probably never exceeding thirty-five miles an hour, it was an incredible thrill. Just as I was becoming mildly comfortable with my steering, an approaching car rattled me.

"Should I stop?" I asked.

"Keep going."

Dad had more confidence than I. Until that moment I'd never noticed how little room there was for two vehicles to pass on the road. Fearing I would crash into the oncoming car, I nervously steered our Chevy to the side, veering so wide that our right tires slipped off the gravel as the other car whooshed by, to my great relief. When we came to a small rise in the road, Dad asked me to stop. I reluctantly exchanged seats with him. Intent now, inspired by my brief turn at the wheel, I watched him handle the car, extending my arms and mimicking his movements at the wheel, unaware that many years would pass before I would settle behind the wheel of a car again. Dad's trips to the Firesteel elevator soon ended. If memory serves, that elevator was destroyed by fire and not rebuilt.

Near the grain elevator in Timber Lake, scattered near the railroad tracks, were a number of petroleum storage tanks lined up like elephants side by side, with a gap between each. Boys my age and older made a game of climbing the metal ladders on the ends of the tanks and leaping from tank to tank, clearing the gaps. It was tricky, at least for kids my age, because the tanks were fairly large and the gap wide enough to present a challenge. There was no possibility for a running start, and we had to land fairly high on the adjoining slope to get traction. Land too low and our leather-soled shoes slipped off the curvature and sent us slithering awkwardly down between the tanks. I banged into the ground often enough, landing on shoulder, rump, or knee, but never broke anything.

What struck me most about that game was my ability to foresee when I'd successfully jump the gap. If I had the slightest doubt before I leaped, I'd end up on the ground. If I thought I'd make it, I'd succeed. It was, I suppose, a hazy glimpse of the process that has become popular among athletes, the process of mentally performing the required physical movements, visualizing each successful muscular effort before actually doing it, and thus increasing the likelihood of success. I don't mean to imply that I harbored such advanced thoughts then, that I had any insight into the psychology of positive thinking. I merely noticed the phenomenon.

My worst day on the tanks came when one of the older boys, I think he was in the sixth grade, brought cigars. After a few jumps, he invited us to take a smoke break. We hunkered down under a tank to light up. Considering the contents of the tanks, it wasn't the smartest place to smoke. I quickly discovered the power of cigars. A queasiness developed in my stomach after a few serious puffs. I squatted there totally miserable, resolved to keep that vile tobacco from my lips, yet I hesitated to stub it out and reveal my weakness. At last, knowing what was coming, I got to my feet and wobbled off without a word to purge myself in private.

Other than a rare ceremonial puff or two in my later youth, I never smoked cigars again.

My first attacks of migraine struck while we lived in Timber Lake. They were classic migraines, throbbing and inevitably intensifying until nothing mattered but the torment in my head. Then came an assault on my stomach, a slimy, sour nausea that fed off my troubled head through invisible loops. The nausea gained force until I, and there is no better word for it in such exquisite misery, puked. I don't recall a warning aura during those initial attacks; either it wasn't yet present, or it passed unnoticed. Later, when I was a first-year medical student studying neuroanatomy, I tried unsuccessfully to figure out which specific sets of neurons and neural connections within my brain evoked the jagged scintillating lines that blurred my vision and warned of the approaching pain. By then I had learned that three aspirin tablets, taken when my aura started, would almost invariably ward off the headache. But being unaware of that simple measure while I lived in Timber Lake, I could expect no relief until I had emptied my stomach's curdled contents. Only then would the pain ease and gradually disappear.

When one such headache started, Dad went to fetch the local doctor who immediately came to attend me. We had no telephone, nor was there one in the feed store. Dad hurried along Main Street and walked into the office of Dr. Harold Stanford, an osteopathic physician. Dr. Stanford brought no pills for me. Rather, he stood behind me as I lay limp on the couch and gently moved my head from side to side. In my miserable state I offered no resistance. After the doctor had manipulated my head long enough to thoroughly relax my neck, he gave a sudden headward jerk. I heard a distinct snap, felt my neck pop. At that instant, and this is no exaggeration, my headache instantly vanished. It was an amazing feat, a piece of magic I wouldn't have believed had I not experienced it. From then on, whenever my migraine called, Dr. Stanford was summoned. Each time his treatment was miraculously effective. Although I later developed a special interest in human physiology, I never have been able to explain satisfactorily how that doctor's magical treatment instantly stopped my headaches.

In Dr. Stanford's back yard were mesh wire cages filled with a slither of rattlesnakes. The doctor hunted snakes and captured them live. It was said that he milked their venom, though that may have been mere rumor. My friends and I occasionally gathered around the cages to study the snakes and watch the tangle of quivering tails transmit their unmistakable warning buzz. Rattlesnakes were common in west-river South Dakota. Dad killed a couple of them around the grain elevator, one inside, on the ramp where the trucks were weighed. When we boys rambled through the prairies surrounding the town, we kept vigilant, especially in rocky areas.

Dr. Stanford at times hunted with my father. Once I rode along when they hunted rabbits at night, using high-powered flashlights attached to their guns. I believe the doctor fed rabbit meat to his snakes.

"Do you like to hunt?" the doctor asked me.

"Yeah, but I only have a BB gun."

Dr. Stanford looked at Dad but spoke to me. "Well, if your dad doesn't mind, you could borrow my pellet gun sometime. When you pump it up, it's nearly as powerful as a .22 rifle."

It sounded terrific to me. Dad said it would be fine with him. Not certain the doctor had really meant it, but eager to use the pellet gun, I knocked on his door one spring morning and asked for his gun. He brought it out, along with a box of pellets and showed me how to use it.

"Have a good hunt," he said, waving me on my way.

With the gun solid and heavy in my hand, I picked up a friend and headed for a patch of prairie southwest of town where new green grass had begun to crowd out last year's brown. We flushed a few jackrabbits from their hiding places and sent them scurrying, but they had little to fear. I wasn't yet marksman enough to hit a bounding target. And after I'd sent a pellet whistling in the general direction of the rabbit, it took a minute or more to reload and pump in a fresh charge of air, time enough for the rabbit to bounce over a hill and disappear, or to hide amid heavier clumps of prairie grass. It was one shot and out.

Though the solid gun in my hands thrilled me, I felt uneasy using it, feared something bad would happen. Before the day was out it did. The gun jammed. I inspected the mechanism, fiddled with it. Cursed it. Had no idea what I'd done to it. I sheepishly returned the damaged goods and apologized in my embarrassment.

"No problem," Dr. Stanford said. "I have another pellet gun, a pistol. You can use that anytime time you want."

"No thanks." I wouldn't make that mistake twice.

But within a week I returned, unable to resist the lure of the pistol. Again I bagged no game. This time I fouled up the pistol. With greater guilt, and feeling totally miserable, I returned the second inoperable gun to the doctor. I apologized and nearly cried.

"Don't worry about it," he said, placing the pistol on his table. "I'm sure it will be easy to fix."

I could tell he meant it. I was stunned. How could he be so kind? Not only did he have the magical skill to abolish my headaches, but his gracious warmth extended to a troublesome kid who had messed up two of his guns. Relieved, and thoroughly enchanted, I turned to go, amazed that there were men of such heroic proportions.

About the time our family moved away from Timber Lake, Dr. Stanford had a stroke of bad luck. A car crash broke his back and caused other severe injuries. The news of his accident struck me with the force of a heavy fist in the stomach. Why him, of all people? After his accident, he returned to his mother's home in Iowa. I often wondered how he coped with his misfortune, how well he healed. He was my Timber Lake hero, Dr. Harold Stanford of Larrabee, Iowa.

World War II blazed on, slowly escalating, pulling the country out of its economic depression, though the effects were little felt in Timber Lake. Our home life was tolerable, but our basic, no-frills existence at times fanned dissatisfaction, a low-spirited numbness that settled on me with increasing frequency. Mother ran the household as best she could on our limited budget and worked constantly: cleaning, washing and mending our clothing, ironing, baking, refusing to give way to her chronic illness which I continued to blindly ignore. Had she complained I might have been more aware of how sick she was, but she stoically plunged on as if she were in the best of health.

I was less able to ignore the tension between our parents, even though they attempted to shield us youngsters from it. Its raw edge was laid open for me one afternoon when I returned from school when Grandpa and Grandma Schafer had come for a visit. I found Mother hunched over on the living room couch, drenched with tears. Grandpa and Grandma stood on either side, consoling her. Although I'd heard not a word of what my mother had said, I knew she had informed them of Dad's shortcomings, of his drinking and gambling. I boiled with instant anger, with my fury wrongly directed toward my mother. How dare she reveal our family's secrets to Grandpa and Grandma? How dare she inform them of Dad's violations? Enraged, I glared at her and stormed outside. Monumentally immature, I failed to see how vulnerable Mother was, how stressful Dad's wasteful ways, that he, not she, was at fault.

Our family shortly before we left Timber Lake

I began to lose my once cheerful outlook. Our marginal life and a skein of petty annoyances wore me down. Plans made fell through. Promises evaporated, unfulfilled. I'd been promised a bicycle from the time I was in the first grade. It never arrived. I told Dad of a used one for sale cheap. There wasn't enough money for that one either. I began to suspect, correctly, that I never would own a bicycle. And I had little hope for my immediate future. I would be fine once I grew up, but I was pretty damned fed up with the present.

Our school planned a pleasant outing. We students were scheduled to travel some twenty miles to Isabel, where we were to compete with students from that town in races and other games. I was thrilled. I'd never been to Isabel. When the day came, we kids gathered in the school yard, charged with excitement. Then I grew uneasy. Something would happen, I thought. Our trip would be canceled. The time came for the bus to arrive. No sign of it. A half hour passed. An hour. Miss Pearson came outside.

"We won't be going to Isabel. The bus has broken down. You may go home."

My shadowy view confirmed, I left the school yard with sagging spirits. But soon afterward, during the summer, came a bright ray of hope. Dad was offered another job, a better one in Aberdeen. It was a double-edged sword for me, one edge cutting me off once more from my friends, the other promising better days. I could handle that. We readied ourselves for the move.

Dad's transfer was by all indications a promotion. He was to work with more seasoned managers in a considerably larger grain elevator complex. Aberdeen had maybe fifteen thousand inhabitants then, Timber Lake fewer than a thousand. The move looked promising. Surely no one expected what actually happened.

CHAPTER 5

Mother had arrived in Timber Lake grandly pregnant. She left town equally so, only days before her fourth baby was due. Dad went directly to his new job in Aberdeen, but the rest of us, Mother, Carol, Betty, and I, stopped for a time in Java to stay with Mother's parents, who only weeks earlier had given up farming and moved into a sturdy two-story home on the southern edge of town. None of us had been born in a hospital, and Mother saw no reason for the added expense this time either. Grandpa and Grandma's bedroom would serve as her delivery room. Soon she went into labor. In those days, before ultrasound or amniocentesis, one didn't know the sex of a baby until it was delivered. The moment of birth carried an additional tension, a pleasant one. The moment arrived. Mother's fourth child was born on August 26, 1942. She named him Gary George. Our family was complete.

Somehow the *Java Herald* failed to record Gary's birth, but it did run the following item in its September 24, 1942 edition: *Mrs.*

George Goetz and children, who have been visiting at the Jacob Schafer home and other relatives for the past few weeks, left Wednesday for their new home at 301 10th Avenue SW, in Aberdeen. Mr. Goetz was recently transferred to the South Dakota Wheat Growers association elevator in Aberdeen.

We had lingered in Java for nearly a month after Gary's birth, to give our depleted mother time to recuperate under her parents' care. Her kidney disease had complicated each of her pregnancies, leaving her weak and exhausted after giving birth. When Mother had sufficiently regained her strength, our grandparents squeezed the five of us, and themselves, into their black 1937 Ford sedan and took us to Aberdeen, cruising eastward on U.S. Highway 12 at Grandpa's absolute top speed, forty miles an hour.

"There goes another darned fool," he muttered, each time a car passed us. Eventually we arrived in Aberdeen.

The house Dad had rented for us was the finest and largest our family ever claimed, just the ticket for the family of a man on the rise. When compared with surrounding homes, it was no more than average, but to us it was perfect. It even provided us with our first street address. I had always been envious of those having real addresses with house numbers and named streets. Such refinements weren't needed in the smaller towns we had lived in. Everyone knew everyone else, knew where they lived. Incoming mail easily reached its target with the simplest of addresses: name, town, and state.

Our new home, its brown exterior freshly painted, had two stories above a full basement. On the first floor were a living room, kitchen, dining room, and enclosed front porch. On the second, four bedrooms and a bathroom, our first home with an indoor toilet. Only those who have depended on outhouses in deep winter will appreciate our excitement over having indoor plumbing. The house even had central heating, another first for us. To complete the miracle, we had a telephone, the only one our family ever had.

School had been in session for some weeks when we arrived, not the best situation for Carol, who was to enroll in kindergarten, or for me. Neither of us relished crashing in after everyone else had settled into their comfortable routines. But on Thursday morning, the day after we had arrived in town, Carol and I set out for our school, Simmons Elementary. Mother had Betty and Baby Gary to care for at home, so I was in charge. We found Carol's room and got her settled in.

I located my fifth grade classroom and nervously opened the door. Every head turned. I announced myself and was thoroughly inspected while the teacher prepared a desk for me. I sat down, relieved to lower my profile, and took stock of the roomful of strangers. Several smiles were beaming my way when a heavyset woman burst into the room and stood before us, her feet making little stamping movements as she surveyed the room.

"Where's the new boy?" she said.

My teacher aimed a finger.

"Stand up," the intruder said. "Come up here."

I immediately disliked her, her antsy feet, her brazen manner, her intrusiveness. Embarrassed by being so rudely singled out, I reluctantly trudged up to join her at the head of the class. Twenty-six pairs of eyes fixed on me.

"Sing America," the woman ordered, shifting her bulk from foot to foot.

What was this? A talent contest I hadn't entered? A crude initiation? And who was this corn-fed witch? How did she know about me? Thoroughly befuddled, I timidly opened my mouth but couldn't make a sound.

"We're waiting," my tormentor said impatiently. When I remained mute, she bellowed, "Sing!"

I'd never been able to sing, never could carry a tune, indeed had heard very little music in my entire life.

"My country, 'tis...," I squawked. My voice locked.

"Keep going."

I couldn't. I stood inert, a miserable heap glowing crimson.

"Help him, class. Everybody sing."

MY COUNTRY, 'TIS OF THEE—. A chorus of sympathetic voices boomed, drowning out my faint efforts, covering for me, carrying the verse to its end. FROM EV'RY MOUNTAIN SIDE LET FREEDOM RING.

Silence. The intruder's feet had stopped trampling the floor. "Flutes?" she said at last, looking at my teacher.

"Flutes," my teacher said.

I slunk back to my seat confused and humiliated. The beefy woman slammed the door behind her. Our music instruction, I was to learn, came in two formats. In one, students from several classes were divided into sections for group training. The best singers were assigned to the glee club, those less talented but able to carry a tune, to the chorus. The remainder, those with voices totally hopeless, were assigned to play song flutes. It was a fine assignment for me, giving me the opportunity to learn to read musical notes and tootle simple songs on my plastic instrument.

The second part of our musical instruction consisted of vocal training in our individual classrooms. For this we were shuffled about. Those with the best voices were seated in the back of each row, the rest of us assigned, like chairs in an orchestra, further forward to our ranked spot. Not surprisingly, I earned a front row seat. When learning a song we first sang it in solfeggio. The pitch pipe drew us somewhat together, we sang in unison. Sol do la fa, mi do re. Then came individual exercises, one row at a time. The best singer in the row would sing the piece solo and then move forward to assist each student in turn, joining voices in a duet before the student soloed. From my front row seat I had the advantage of listening to each melody several times and thus became familiar with the tune before my turn came. My student tutor was a lovely girl, Janet, whose voice was velvet in my ear. I began to look forward to singing with Janet, her tone holding mine on key, her shoulder electric against mine. As the year progressed, my vocal efforts surprisingly surpassed those of several students behind me. I was promoted backward seat by seat until my assigned place was near the middle, a progression attributable less to ability than to my efforts to please, my infatuation with Janet.

When Carol and I found our way to Simmons Elementary on our first morning, I tried to prepare her for her walk home, anticipating that she would be dismissed from her classes earlier than I and thus would need to find her way home alone. From our house on the corner of Third Street and Tenth Avenue, Simmons lay a few blocks directly south on Third Street. To return home Carol simply needed to reverse our morning course and head northward. That would take her home in less than ten minutes. But she was only five and in a strange town. When dismissed, she became confused and wandered in the wrong direction, heading east rather than north, possibly because she left the school through a different door from the one we had entered. Helpless in the unfamiliar territory, panic rising, she began to wail, attracting the attention of a woman who took her into her home and offered her cookies and milk before telephoning our mother. When I returned from school Mom sent me to pick her up. Carol and I detoured past Simmons to reorient her before heading for home. After that she kept her bearings as reliably as a homing pigeon.

While at Simmons I was introduced to soccer, a sport I'd never heard of. Simmons was well ahead of the national curve;

soccer wasn't a common pastime in our country then. We boys flocked to the soccer field during our recesses and flew over it in a tangle of arms and legs until we were called back to our classes. A few players excelled, particularly Lou, a classmate who dribbled the ball with consummate skill and scored at will. I never approached Lou's knack with the ball, but he and I saw eye to eye on one important matter. We both admired Janet. We compared notes, talked about our dream girl endlessly, whetted our appetites, decided to act. One Saturday morning we rang the doorbell of her home.

"Yes, boys?" Her mother looked down at us.

We had prepared for that eventuality. "We'd like to take Janet to a movie," Lou said. "Would that be okay with you?"

Janet's mother was equally prepared. "That's very nice of you, but Janet isn't old enough to go out with boys. Maybe when she's in high school..."

She let the sentence dangle. High school? That would be years from now. I sensed Janet listening beyond the open door and felt a surge of excitement. Though our mission failed, I floated home with modest satisfaction. Janet *knew*.

Those first few months on Tenth Avenue were idyllic. Dad had a responsible job. Mother contentedly cared for her family with little strain. We were a united family and, from all external appearances, normal. It was a special time, those early months in Aberdeen, a time of apparent normalcy, a tantalizing glimpse at what might have been, at what I naively considered to be our future.

One Sunday morning in early winter - late 1942 or early 1943 - we awoke to a fresh snowfall. Cozy beneath my quilt, I heard Mom and Dad whispering in their bedroom, Carol and Betty giggling in theirs, Gary gooing in his crib near Mom and Dad, a fine morning to lounge in bed, but I had work to do. A neighborhood boy, Bill, and I had planned for this first snowy weekend. I dressed quickly and threw on jacket, stocking cap, overshoes, and gloves and met Bill at his house. We went door to door lugging snow shovels, offering our services. I was amazed by the heavy demand for our work. We scraped pathways clean and collected whatever each person chose to give us, usually a dollar or two. By the time hunger and cold drove us home we had earned several dollars apiece. I'd never earned more than a dime, a quarter on the outside, for any kind of work. Now I had dollars. Dollars to spend. I was newly rich.

Bill and I added to our modest comic book collections - those featuring Superman or Batman and Robin were my favorites - and traded issues back and forth. We splurged on movies at the Capitol, or the Lyric, or the Orpheum. We watched Gary Cooper in Sergeant York, James Cagney in Yankee Doodle Dandy. But the most pleasure for my money came from the luscious chocolate malts at Lacy's Dairy Bar. Bill introduced me to those wickedly thick and delicious treats. The malts were served at the counter in their gleaming metal canisters along with a large clear glass. After the glass had been poured full, the canister contained yet half as much. I became addicted and slugged down three or four before my earnings ran out. The malts cost a quarter as I recall. I felt charmed and wondered at times if my sudden good fortune was a dream.

When I returned home from my Sunday snow shoveling, Mom and Dad were having coffee in bed, reading the Sunday *Aberdeen American-News*, waiting for me to report my earnings. Afterward Mom prepared bacon and eggs and pancakes and we gathered in our dining room, Gary with a bottle in his buggy, Betty in her high chair, Dad, Mom, Carol, and I around the table. Our family momentarily at its pinnacle. Never again would the six of us be so snugly linked, so much a family. I was ten then, soon to be eleven, too green to spot the erosion beneath the surface.

School was my main problem. Within days of being assigned to flutes, I was placed in the middle of three reading groups. Now I knew that I couldn't sing, that I belonged in flutes, but I also knew that I could read as well as anyone in the class. When my mother met with my teacher during their first scheduled parent-teacher conference, she asked about my placement in reading. My teacher glossed over it, saying there was little difference between the two upper groups, that Mother shouldn't be concerned. I knew better. And I didn't like it. My life was no longer untainted by opinion. I grew increasingly judgmental, especially of those who were unfair to me.

I encountered other minor strains at school. For an early art assignment we were to select from our school books a picture or drawing that we'd like to copy freehand. I'd had no meaningful instruction in art, hadn't yet learned to appreciate it, had little interest in drawing. The rules regarding that particular assignment were simple: after making our choice we were to show it to our teacher and get her permission before beginning our sketch. I found a fine illustration of a sailing ship, one I thought I could handle. I took it to my teacher.

"That's fine, Kenneth, but Michael has chosen the same one."

"Okay, I'll find another one."

"Not so fast. I think you two should have a contest to see which one gets to draw the ship."

"No, I don't want to. I'd rather draw another picture." I wondered why both of us couldn't draw the same ship. It seemed a simple solution.

"I've decided. You two will have a contest on the black board."

I'd seen some of Michael's drawings and knew he drew much better than I. Surely my teacher knew it too.

"I'll find another picture," I said. "I don't want to draw the ship."

"Go to the board please. Michael, will you please go to the board with Kenneth and draw the ship you've chosen? I'll judge the contest and decide who wins."

We stood before the blackboard, my competitor to my left. He swept his chalk in graceful arcs to form the bow, worked backward to the stern, filled his sails with air. I scrawled away and sneaked glances at his fine sketch, hoping to steal ways to improve my own pitiful ship. I knew what the rest of the kids were thinking. Goetz can't sing and he can't draw. What else can't he do? We stood there forever, Michael sending his great ship speeding through ocean waves, I scratching wavering white lines.

In the end my teacher judged the contest a draw, declaring that both of us could draw the ship. It had been contrived from the beginning. Who was she kidding? Being first embarrassed, then patronized by having my sketch judged equal to Michael's, I was beginning to dislike my teacher. But I was too polite then, too compliant, to openly display my hostility. I sketched my imperfect ship on paper, seething, adding ugly blemishes fore and aft.

A set of railroad tracks crossed Third Street between Simmons Elementary and our house. Trains occasionally blocked our way. One mild winter afternoon, a grimy layer of snow thawing beneath our feet, Bill and I neared the tracks on our way home from school. A large dark car came inching along from the north. I paid little attention until the car veered sluggishly toward us, crowding the extreme right side of the road, coming within a yard of me. The driver's eyes were on me. I wasn't alarmed. I idly reached out and brushed the car's front fender with my index finger as it passed by, streaking the winter grime collected there. Bill and I had crossed the tracks before I realized that the big car had stopped. A large man climbed out of the driver's seat, his suit fitting fashionably over his bulk.

"Come here, you," he said. His voice was harsh.

"Who?" I said.

"You. Come here."

I couldn't understand why the man was so riled. Or why his female passenger glared. I didn't want to go to him, but I did.

"Get into the car," he said.

"What for?"

"Don't talk back to me. Get into the car." He opened the back door. It was the last thing I wanted to do, but I had been taught to obey adults. I nervously got in.

"What's your name?"

"Kenneth."

"Your last name."

"Goetz"

"Where do you live?"

I told him. Maybe he was going to drive me home and tell Mother whatever I had done.

"Do you go to Simmons?"

"Yes."

He shifted into gear and got the car moving. Kept it heading south, toward the school. He glared at me through the rear-view mirror. "Don't you know better than to touch a car driving on the road? You could have been killed."

I wanted to ask him why he had driven toward us. But I didn't say a word. Besides, he was crazy to think I could have been killed. He had been traveling way too slowly. I easily could have jumped out of the way. When we reached Simmons, he stopped in the school yard.

"Who's your teacher?"

My God, he was going to tell my teacher about this? What for? Because I drew a streak on his dirty car?

"Please, mister, I didn't mean anything by it." I hated to grovel, but I didn't want my teacher involved. She was the first teacher who hadn't treated me well, and I didn't want to further erode my position. But the man grabbed my arm and dragged me into the school, leaving his wife in the car. I couldn't help myself. My eyes began to water. My teacher knew the man and immediately stood up when we entered.

"This youngster," he said, squeezing my arm and hurting it, "rushed into the road and marked my car when I drove by."

I couldn't believe it. This big guy standing tall in his expensive suit, lying through his teeth, just to get me into trouble. Looking back now, to give him the benefit of the doubt, maybe he had tried to teach us a lesson as he drove by, to get out of the way of cars. When I didn't follow his script and scramble away, and when I had the audacity to touch his car, he flew into a rage.

My teacher listened to the case against me and frowned. She treated the big guy with great respect. She told him I was new at Simmons this year, that I had moved from Timber Lake.

"These small town kids don't know much," he said, scowling at me. "Now get out of here." He gave me a little shove.

I turned to go, burning with malice. From his conversation with my teacher as I was leaving, I learned who he was, a rather prominent citizen. His name appeared now and then in the local daily, the *Aberdeen American-News*. When I read about him in the newspaper a time or two afterward, I wondered how many others knew, as I did, how treacherous he was, how black his despicable heart.

When I told other kids about my brush with absolute authority, they asked why I hadn't run away when the man called me. "He'd never have caught you," they said, offering a truism worth pondering.

I wish I could remember why Dad stopped working at the grain elevator in Aberdeen. He lasted only a few months. Did he get angry and quit? Maybe. More likely he was fired, maybe for drinking on the job, though that is pure speculation. Whatever the reason, he was out of work by midwinter, a shock to me. My father, who had many talents, had failed to make the grade. He had been found wanting. His setback troubled me, troubled my mother. We, or at least I, had expected more of him. He looked for work elsewhere and, after a week or two of searching, found work with a home insulating crew, drilling holes in houses and blowing loose insulation into walls and attics. The crew worked mostly in small Dakota towns, and Dad often was gone for weeks at a time.

One day in early spring two men wearing suits and ties knocked at our door. My mother was in the kitchen. I opened the door.

"Is your father here?" one said.

"No, but my mother is." I called for her.

When she came into the living room, I saw I had made a mistake. I ran upstairs and listened just beyond the stairway.

The men wasted no time with preliminaries. "How is it," one demanded, "that you can pay another finance company but can't pay ours?"

I couldn't hear Mother's soft answer.

"Where is your husband?"

Again I couldn't hear what Mother said. The men's voices rose, sarcastic voices, demanding to know when she would pay up. "We'll be back," one said.

"Why did you open the door?" Mother asked, visibly upset when I came down the stairs.

"I didn't know who they were." And I hadn't known we had borrowed money from a finance company. There were other things I didn't know. Aunt Ella later told me that Dad had come to her and Uncle Ted shortly before we moved to Aberdeen, telling them he needed money. Ella and Ted were farming then. They loaned him five hundred dollars and drove him to Aberdeen at his request. He told them he'd probably stay there and get a job.

"He was very nervous," Ella said. "When we got to Aberdeen, he had us drop him off on a corner of Main Street and asked us to meet him there in half an hour. He was in hot water for something, had to pay someone off, but he never let on who it was. When he got back in the car, he said he'd decided to drive back to the farm with us. I don't remember how he got to our farm or back to Timber Lake. Your mother paid back the loan over the next few years, sending ten dollars or whatever when she could. We didn't know then how little you had or we'd have told her not to send anything."

From Ella's description, it seems likely that Dad had already tapped one of the finance companies and was in arrears. Ella had a postscript to her story. After we'd settled in Aberdeen, she once drove down with her parents to visit us. She remembers that Grandpa Schafer brought along some of his home-made sausage, one of Mom's favorites.

"While we were there, your mother had to make a payment," Ella said. "She apologized for having to do it while we were there. She was tense. I went with her while Grandpa and Grandma stayed home with you kids. We walked a long way, I think to the uptown area. She gave someone in a small office the cash."

Soon after being confronted by the men from the finance company, Mother had bad news for me.

"We have to move," Kenny. "We can't afford to live here anymore." I knew we hadn't heard from Dad in weeks, but I hadn't expected this.

"Where will we go?"

"Someplace cheaper."

"Close to here?"

"I don't know."

She looked through the newspaper, circled ads for rental houses, and sent me to survey them. I looked but didn't like any of them. I liked where we were. I told her none were any good. She knew I was stalling and had me stay with Carol, Betty, and Gary while she looked around herself. She found one, a house on Second Street located a mile or so to the north. It was available cheap but came with a heavy obligation. An invalid, an elderly man, lived upstairs. Mother was to care for him.

I've blanked out all memory of our move. I don't think Dad came back to help us. I don't know where Mother got the money to move us. But just that quickly we exchanged our fine brown house for a rundown white one.

School was still in session. To get all the way to Simmons on time I had to scurry every morning. When I came in late, my teacher frowned. I didn't tell her we had moved. I was afraid she'd insist that I transfer to another school. I wasn't about to barge into another roomful of strangers for the final few weeks of the school year. Our move forced Carol to drop kindergarten. The hike to Simmons was too much for her small legs.

Nursing the old man upstairs was a full-time job. Mother gave him soups and puddings, spoon feeding him. He was irascible, a tyrant who summoned her frequently by thumping his cane on the floor. Our ceiling thumped when he was hungry, thumped when he fouled his bed, thumped for every demand, thumped day and night. Mother trudged up and down the stairs. Up and down. I helped her at times and came to detest his thumping, his stinking room. The stench from his bedpan and his soiled sheets drifted down to us like heavy fog. Mother wore herself out cleaning up his messes, putting up with his abuse. She was frailer now, though she never slowed her pace. It took a month, maybe two, for her to reach her limit.

"We have to move, Kenny," she said, exhausted.

I tried to be optimistic. "Can we go back to where we were?" She didn't bother to answer. Or smile.

Again she circled newspaper ads and sent me out scouting. One ad, marked with a star as her first choice, listed a house out west on Fifth Avenue, near Lincoln school. The small house didn't look bad from the outside, but I didn't want to move there. Lincoln had a bad reputation among those of us at Simmons. I had no intention of going to Lincoln next year. And the house was too far from Simmons for Carol and me to hike the distance day after day, especially during bad weather. Besides, someone would discover we had moved and make us transfer anyway. I reported back to Mother.

"It's no good."

She went to look for herself. It was, she concluded, far better than where we were. It had no tyrant to wear her out.

So we moved again, the third time in less than a year. It was early summer. The boys I met along Fifth Avenue were friendly, most a year or two older than I. The first one I spoke with told me he couldn't wait for fall to arrive. He didn't strike me as the bookish sort.

"For school to start?"

"Naw, for the sweet corn season. We make good money then."

"Do you think I could get a job too?"

The boy stared at me. "Are you nuts?" he said. "We don't work. We swipe the corn. We watch a couple of big gardens. When the corn's ready, we bag it and sell it door to door."

It sounded risky to me and I told him so.

"Some people may be suspicious," he said, "but nobody can prove we stole it. Besides we sell it cheap. We've got good customers who wait every year for us to show up with our sweet corn."

The fellow was a mover. He noticed we didn't have a car or garden tools, that our garage was empty. "Could we play cards in there?"

"Sure."

A few days later he showed up with two buddies and two seventh grade girls. "Let's play," he said, pulling a pack of cards from his pocket.

The six of us sat on the floor of the garage while he explained his rules for the game, strip poker. All losers of each hand would remove one item of clothing. He dealt. He won the first hand. We five losers each removed a shoe and placed it in front of us. I smelled someone's feet. One of the girls giggled. Our leader dealt again. One of his buddies won. Dealt again. I won.

I was carefully keeping score. Each girl had lost two shoes and one sock. This was getting interesting. I noticed the dealer do strange things as he collected the cards. He shuffled the deck and dealt again. He won with three jacks. The girls were now barefoot. I had a sock in reserve. I watched the dealer more closely, saw him clumsily manipulate the cards. It wasn't fair.

"Hey," I said, "what's going on?" Three boys glared at me. I paused to reconsider the situation. After one more hand two blouses would be removed.

"You want something?"

"Naw." The dealer gave me a full house. Way to go!

Now both girls were giggling but willing to follow the rules. A little fumbling with buttons and off came two blouses. I gaped at two underfilled brassieres. There was no need to object right now, was there? I wondered what kind of underpants the girls wore.

"What's going on in there?" A woman peered in through the garage window, her hands cupped around her eyes. It was the mother of one of the girls, who apparently had seen us come in and close the door. She barged in and screamed at her partly-undressed daughter. Then she screamed at us boys, mainly me for being the host. Her arrival saved me. I didn't have to object to the dealer's cheating, which I surely would have after another hand or two.

My new acquaintances had hoodlum instincts. One day the neighborhood leader, a short, athletic boy a few years older than I, described a house ripe for burglarizing. The man and woman who lived there worked during the day; their kids were away. I wanted no part of it.

"Are you going to rat on us?" the leader asked me. The others regarded me with suspicion.

"No."

"You'd better come with us."

I considered my options and chose the least dangerous one. I went with them. Our target was a nearby house with a white clapboard exterior, located on the corner of a block. We slouched along the sidewalk on the north side of the house, casing it, then along its east side, casing it some more. On our leader's orders a small fellow younger than I slipped over to the south side of the house. He crouched down, forced open a basement window, and dropped through. In less than a minute he had unlocked the back door and let us in, all this in mid-afternoon. There were five of us. None of the others were trembling. The first thing I spotted was an apple pie on the kitchen counter, three slices remaining.

"Wow," I said, losing my nervousness and heading for it. I hadn't eaten that day.

"Don't be an idiot," our leader said. "Touch that pie and they'll know someone was here."

I was hungry enough to risk that but not starved enough to antagonize my companions. As I stood sadly in the kitchen, swallowing saliva while my stomach rumbled, the others fanned through the house. They took a few dollars, nothing else that I recall. I, scared and shaking, took nothing. All I wanted was a slice of the forbidden pie, or all of it. Someone closed the basement window. We left through the back door, to my great relief. It was my only break-in. A clean job.

I was ravenous at the time because we had run out of food the day before, having eaten the last of our bread with sugar sprinkled on it. There was not a thing in the house to eat. Mother fed Gary sugar water in his bottle. He lay in his crib and gazed at the ceiling, wondering what sort of world he had come into. Carol saw two girls eating an orange as they walked along the sidewalk. Driven by overpowering hunger, she picked up the peelings and ate them after the girls had gone.

We hadn't heard from Dad for a couple of weeks. Money had run out. We had gotten by as long as we did because I'd been able to sell my comic books, picking up small change for my collection. I didn't mind selling them. I practically knew them by heart. But I had no more comics to sell.

For Christmas I had been give a pair of ice skates, a fine pair of hockey skates from Sears, two-tone leather, black and tan. Dad still worked for the grain elevator then. I had skated with a friend at Simmons earlier in the year and remembered his skates gave him blisters. Maybe he'd be interested in mine. I hurried to see him, a half-hour walk, pretending I'd stopped by just to say hello. After some small talk I asked whether he'd bought new skates. He hadn't.

"I'm thinking of selling mine," I said.

"How much?"

"I don't know, maybe five dollars."

"I'd have to see them."

Encouraged, I walked home to get them. An hour later I showed him how fine my skates were. He looked and decided not to buy. I didn't understand. My skates were practically new. But it was early summer, not the best season to sell ice skates. I dropped the price to four dollars. I was hungry.

"Nope."

"Three dollars?"

"I don't think so."

Never negotiate from weakness. Never negotiate when hungry. "Two-fifty?"

"Okay." He went to get the money. On my way home I passed near Lacy's Dairy Bar and thought of the marvelous malts Bill and I used to get there. Pulled by the lure of icy chocolate, my feet took control and walked me past the store, stopped me and backtracked. I stood at the door struggling. I wanted to walk away but my pockets had been empty too long, the temptation overwhelming. I went in. Ordered. The frosty drink was incredibly delicious, sliding quickly into my shrunken stomach. I would have enjoyed it even more had each icy mouthful not been laced with guilt.

I couldn't admit what I'd done. Couldn't reveal my shameful selfishness. I lied to Mother. I knew Gary needed milk, so I stopped at the corner grocery near our house and bought a quart. And I thought we needed bread, so I bought a loaf.

"Look what I brought," I told Mother. "I got two dollars and a quarter for my skates and bought bread and milk." I handed her the change, hoping the food would distract her from the catch in my deceitful voice.

Mother's agitation twisted her face. She had intended to bake something, to make the money go further. She had wanted flour, not bread. And she angrily let me know it.

"I can take it back," I said. She made a short list and sent me back with the bread and the change to get what she wanted. Afterward she baked and we ate our fill. But I knew it was a temporary fix. I could think of nothing else to sell.

Not long after I sold my ice skates someone told Mother that Dad was in town. I don't know who told her that, or how the word was passed. The informant indicated that Dad often could be found in a certain saloon that she named. Mom dispatched me to the establishment to ask if anyone knew George Goetz. I went at once, knowing he wouldn't be there and wanting to ease Mother's mind. The saloon, I've forgotten its name, was located just west of Main Street on either Second or Third Avenue, on the south side of the street. The place had a run-down look, a bare wooden floor, a long bar facing the entrance, dark wooden booths with high backs along the east wall. It was nearly empty at midday, no one on the bar stools. I quickly scanned the booths. My jaw dropped.

In one of the middle booths, with a half-empty schooner before him, sat my father, talking with a man and woman seated opposite. All three were smoking. I stood dumbfounded. We were starving at home and there he sat, drinking beer and smoking less than two miles from where we lived in misery. He had to be paying for a room somewhere, eating regular meals, buying cigarettes, and filling himself with beer. He knew we had no money, no food. Didn't he care? It may be difficult to understand, but my astonishment, and my flaring anger, gave way to an odd sense of relief, much like a seagoing passenger might feel when reaching for a scrap of flotsam after his ship has gone down.

Dad was equally astonished to see me. After he collected himself, he called me over and invited me to sit beside him. I stood stiffly beyond his reach.

"When are you coming home?" I asked.

He glanced at his two companions, visibly embarrassed. "Soon," he said.

I had nothing more to say. I was confused, trying to understand how he could have deserted us. I turned and stumbled out, wondering for just a moment whether we had done something wrong, something that made him leave us. No. Absolutely not. It wasn't our fault. I hurried home to give my report to Mother, who gave no sign of surprise, only sorrow. Dad came home late that night, after we all were in bed. I was glad to see him the next morning but unable to warm to him. He provided money for groceries, stayed a few days, then left again, telling us he had another insulating job out of town, leaving a few dollars on the table as he walked out the door.

The larger world had become irrelevant. To our southwest, in a corner of South Dakota I would never see while I lived there, George, Thomas, Abraham, and Theodore gazed out from Mount Rushmore with freshly-chiseled eyes. A distant war blazed on. Rommel was routed from Africa. The Pacific was aflame. Marines hoisted our flag on Guadalcanal. Men we knew slightly died in action. Yet these events were dwarfed by our immediate concerns. Gasoline was rationed, as were canned foods and shoes, meat and cheese. What did that matter to us?

Our situation had never been darker. We couldn't go on as we had. Somehow Mother would have to take charge. To aggressively demand more from Dad, or to alert our relatives of our plight. To do something. Or I'd have to steal, get my hands on money one way or another. We had to bring food into the house for our five mouths. We would have no future if we starved to death. One of us needed to act. I don't know why Mother was so passive, why she didn't take action and demand more from Dad. Did her illness break her spirit? She was a country girl, reared in the shadow of a Lutheranism that demanded sacrifice, the acceptance of one's lot, faith in God for salvation. A graduate of a small high school, married at twenty, she was inexperienced in rough and tumble games, not adept at confrontation. And, at age thirty-five, far sicker than I realized. She needed someone to care for her, to comfort her. But her lot was to give, not to receive.

I wish I'd been more supportive, had been more alert to her needs. I think she reached out for solace one day, though I didn't recognize it then. She called me aside one evening, told me she was going to bleed that night, that she would put newspapers on her bed and would need my help with the cleanup in the morning. My street education hadn't covered menstruation; I thought the bleeding was a sign of her worsening illness. Bleeding sounded bad. I worried, too scared myself to offer whatever comfort I might have given her. She had no one to support her, no money for tampons or pads. I don't know why she didn't wrap herself. Maybe she did. I fretted through the night. The next morning, not knowing what the mess was, I helped her clean it up, throwing a sackful of wadded-up newspapers into the trash, emptying buckets of bloody water down the toilet. The blood told me how ill she really was. Though it was a false sign, one I had misinterpreted, it nevertheless correctly alerted me to how sick my mother really was.

It may have been pride that kept Mother from throwing our burden to our relatives, yet I think she was ready to do it. I thought of plotting more break-ins with the neighborhood gang, and even wondered if I could pull one off by myself. A Lutheran belief in honesty is hard to break, but we had to eat to survive.

Into this desperate situation came a sudden salvation, and from an unexpected source. Dad surprised us one day by coming home with money for food, and exciting news. Mr. Larson, our former neighbor in Onida, had refurbished the Onida movie theater with a silent partner. He wanted Dad to be the projectionist. Given that reprieve, our spirits miraculously rejuvenated, we prepared to move back to Onida.

CHAPTER 6

Onida in the summer of 1943, at the midpoint of our country's involvement in World War II, was much as we had left it in peacetime three years earlier. We rented a comfortable two-bedroom house on Main Street, a block south of the lower end of the business district, and settled in.

Dad reported to Mr. Larson for work and effortlessly mastered his responsibilities in the projection booth, operating the two carbon-arc projectors, adjusting them for optimal light intensity, loading reels of film into the projectors and synchronizing the shift from one projector to the other when showing multiple reels of the main feature. The newly remodeled theater, its glossy, brightly-colored exterior panels gleaming over the sidewalk, was the jewel of Main Street. Inside, new heavy drapes separated the tiny refurbished lobby from the theater seats. General maintenance and cleaning of the facility fell to Dad, as did management of its day-to-day activities. My father! It was a fine opportunity for him, and, as it turned out, for me.

115

Mr. Larson offered me the job of taking tickets and selling popcorn. I jumped at the chance without bothering to ask what my pay would be. The Social Security Act had become law eight years earlier, and I, feeling quite grown up, applied for my social security number.

"The good thing about the system," Dad told me, "is that the money you pay into it goes to a special fund that builds up until you retire. It's like money in the bank. And your social security number can never be used for identification. It's part of the law. See, it's even printed on the card."

My theater job was great, taking tickets and tearing them in half, popping corn in the theater's popper with its four clear-glass sides, scooping the freshly-popped kernels into white bags, one size only, knowing the tantalizing aroma would entice customers. I felt useful and important. And I was being paid, a trivial wage to be sure, but I'd gladly have worked for less.

After the lights had dimmed I stood inside the draped doorway munching my free popcorn, my duties largely fulfilled for the evening, and gave my attention to the latest newsreel, watching the flickering cone of light from Dad's projection booth transform itself into our soldiers battling the Germans in Italy, or MacArthur's troops advancing in the Solomons. Caught up in the shattering force of shells, the occasional glimpses of torn flesh, I swelled with patriotic fervor as the strong narrative voice praised the bravery of our troops while leaving no doubt how evil our enemy was. I loathed the enemy, the wild-looking Hitler with his unkempt slab of oily hair, his ridiculous mustache. I hated his partners in crime, Mussolini and Hirohito.

Often I slipped up to the projection booth to keep Dad company while he unpacked reels of film and threaded them into the projectors. Though the remodeled theater looked great, the projection equipment was old and temperamental and required constant monitoring, frequent adjustments of the carbon arcs, a sharp eye on the focus. I would sit beside one of the small observation windows and peep through to follow the action on screen, or to check the vague silhouettes of my friends in the front rows. I had my first glimpse of Bing Crosby through that window, heard him croon "White Christmas." In the rare times when Mother substituted for one of the Larsons at the ticket window, it was a family affair, three of us working together. Life was good. I had a few coins to spend. Our family once again had stabilized. Though Dad wasn't paid handsomely, he had a responsible job. If he would stay away from alcohol, we would be fine.

I was eager for the school term to start. This time I would rejoin former friends, not face strangers, upon enrolling. On the first day of classes, Carol and I walked together to the elementary school, where I proudly directed her into the room on the south side of the first floor, the same room that I had occupied when I was her age. From there I took the stairway to the room directly above it, where practically all of my former classmates were gathered.

Physically, I had always considered myself average: average height, average weight, average speed, average strength, average looks. So it came as a great shock when Mother, early in the school year, told me that a woman had complimented her on her handsome son and his long eyelashes, the longest she'd ever seen on a boy. Gary was a toddler then, and I had spoken with the woman a day or two earlier, so I knew which of Mother's sons she referred to. The woman's opinion intrigued me. I, and my friends, had noticed our pubescent gears beginning to engage, our voices deepening, certain enlargements.

Our physical changes pumped new energy into our classroom. We eyed the girls with new interest. They eyed us back. We brushed lightly against them as we passed their desks. We exchanged notes, tame ones at first, innocent, tentative. Then we upped the ante, braving a new word or two, a wrinkle of meaning, a snippet of salaciousness, gradually shifting the line we allowed ourselves to cross. As we racheted up the stakes, adding randy humor, exciting ourselves with our efforts, I became addicted to our notes, passing mine on, reading those of others, smirking, imagining. Only the slimmest list of words remained taboo. We didn't talk boy to girl in that way, but words on paper were okay. I threw myself into the game, straining the limits of my inventiveness, creating stories in doggerel, exposing my sinning protagonists to frightful peril. Our excellent teacher, Mrs. Johnson, a woman I admired and respected, seemed not to notice our illicit activity.

One day I scaled new heights and filled an entire page with relatively well-rhymed smut. Proud of the modest pinnacle I'd attained, anxious to display my cleverness, I tore the page from my tablet and folded it as tightly as a full page of paper can be folded. My desk was at the very back of a middle row. A fifth grade girl, Georgia, who reportedly had a crush on me, sat to my left. Our teacher sat at her desk helping another student, her head lowered. I caught Georgia's attention and stretched out my arm to her.

"What's going on back there?"

"Nothing." I had mouthed the word, but it didn't sound like my voice.

"Bring that up here, Kenneth."

"It's nothing." The thought of her reading my foul trash nearly stopped my heart.

"You heard me. Bring it up here. Now."

I stood up, numb with shame. She would consider it disgusting. I should have eaten the incriminating paper on the spot, should have torn it to shreds, should have run screaming from the room. But I obediently shuffled forward, my face scarlet, and handed the thing to her.

She slipped it into her purse and turned her attention back to the pupil she'd been helping. My mind whirred. I told myself she'd forget about the note and toss it out when cleaning her purse, without reading it. Fat chance. I had a natural talent for guilt. And this time I deserved every stab of it. I worried all afternoon. All the next morning.

"Give me your attention, please," Mrs. Johnson said on the next afternoon, driving a stiletto through my spine. I knew what was coming. My face flamed.

"I've seen a lot of notes floating around for the past week. I want that to end. Right now. I know what you've been writing about, and it's shocking." Her eyes cut directly to me. "You should be ashamed of yourselves."

I was, in fact, the object of all eyes. Everyone knew whose note had been read, though not its contents. Only two knew what I had written, my teacher and I. I had been a favorite of hers. And I had humiliated myself. I had let her down.

A year later, after our class had moved over to the high school building which housed the seventh and eighth grade classroom, Mrs. Johnson came to visit us. As I recall she had moved to another town during the summer. Our seventh grade teacher, Miss Trythall, told her that I'd been the only student to achieve a perfect score in arithmetic that day. Mrs. Johnson smiled at me. When I returned her smile, my mind flew back, as perhaps hers did, to the contents of the note we once had shared. What had she really thought, I wondered, when she read of my sinning protagonists, their lustful behavior?

Kenneth in Onida

In Onida I accelerated my smoking. Practically all of us boys in Onida carried cigarettes. We smoked when circumstances permitted, inhaled, learned silly tricks. I perfected the trick of flipping a lighted butt into my mouth using only tongue, lips, and teeth, the glowing tip suspended just above my tongue. For effect I would close my lips and seal the cigarette inside before flipping it out again and taking another drag, my hands all the while behind my back, a trivial talent I prized in that phase of my life. All of our fathers smoked, mine Lucky Strikes, other fathers Camels or Chesterfields. We youngsters usually opted for

Avalons, which sold for fifteen cents for a pack of twenty, a nickel cheaper than the main brands, or Wings, also fifteen cents a pack, and a longer cigarette.

"I hear you're smoking," Dad said one evening. We twelve-year-olds weren't brazen. We smoked on the sly, out of sight of adults. I wondered which one of my friends had squealed on me. And why.

"Not I," I said. It was a reflex denial. I expected Dad to hammer away, to crowd me with questions until I came clean, but he seemingly bought my denial and dropped the subject.

It was the briefest conversation, by itself of no obvious import, yet it shaped my life from that moment forward. The next time I lit up I thought of what I had done. I had lied to my father. Not that I hadn't lied before, but this was a weighty lie, uncalled for. If I were man enough to smoke, I should be man enough to admit it. I stubbed out my cigarette and announced to my two smoking companions that I was quitting - no more tobacco for me. When I followed through and actually quit, I became a novelty, the only kid in our pack who didn't smoke. I missed the buzz at first, but not enough to break my pledge.

Thinking back, I'm sure it was Mother who tipped off Dad about my smoking. She didn't smoke and surely smelled the reek of my clothes. But she let Dad handle it. Thanks to their intervention, I gave up the weed at age twelve, before it tightened its addictive clutch on me. Had I succumbed to lifelong tobacco use, and had I been afflicted with emphysema, or heart disease, or lung cancer, I could not in good conscience have screamed at the tobacco companies and filed suit against them, claiming I didn't know the danger of cigarettes. Even as boys we called them coffin nails, or cancer sticks, just as our fathers did.

"We're going to the Larson's place tonight after the show," Mother said with a cheerful smile while primping before her dresser mirror, adding a touch of rose to her lips, powder to her cheeks. Though it was Saturday evening, Mother wore her "Sunday" dress, made of rayon I think, a delicate fabric with a floral print. It was far from new but looked good on her. "And Mr. Blank will be there too."

"Blank" was the silent theater partner of the Larsons and lived out of town; I can't recall his name. Mother had always liked the Larsons, another reason she was thrilled by the invitation. It would be a rare social evening for her. Dad often went out to play cards and drink beer, but Mom usually stayed home. They had gone dancing in Onida a time or two, major outings for her, but I can't recall much else they did together. Mother gave a happy wave as she left with Dad.

The next morning I found them having coffee in the kitchen.

"How were the Larsons?" I asked.

"Okay," Dad said. Mother's eyes were red, her jaw tight.

I didn't learn what had happened until Monday afternoon when I came home from school. Dad was out somewhere, Carol and Betty were across the street playing with the Stewart kids, and Gary was napping in his crib.

"What happened?" I asked Mother, who was busily sorting laundry.

She sighed and put the laundry back into the basket and walked slowly into the living room and sat down on the couch. I trailed along and sat beside her.

It had been a setup, she told me, an ambush. The Larsons had become dissatisfied with Dad's work, or perhaps his attitude, and had changed their opinion of him entirely. For weeks they had systematically collected their grievances and organized them for an evening's sport. They assembled the cast, the unsuspecting George and Emma, Mr. Blank, and themselves, in their living room and attacked without warning, lobbing round after round of vicious accusations at George. He had done this. He had failed to do that. I don't recall the specifics. His many misdeeds, like the name of the Larson's partner who sat silently listening, are lost in time. But clearly for the Larsons my father had become, like a penny flipped into the air to land heads or tails, unpredictable, and of little monetary value. He was sacked. All of this influenced me in ways I didn't realize then. Rather than trying to be like my father, I began to differentiate myself from him, to view him as the sort of person I didn't want to become.

I didn't blame the Larsons for firing Dad. What infuriated me was their underhanded attack on my mother. They had lured her to their home on the pretext that it would be a social evening and had belittled and embarrassed her, a total innocent.

"I wanted to sink right through the floor," Mother said, unable to hold the tears back. She had held the Larsons in high regard and could not understand why they had turned on her, could not fathom why she too had been condemned.

I don't know whether Dad defied the Larsons, whether he defended Mother. He should have. I was so incensed by the reprehensible deception that only gradually did I realize that I too had lost my job. I was never officially fired, but it was over. Not wanting to set eyes on either of the Larsons again, I avoided the movie theater for months afterward. When I recovered enough to slink back in, I hid my envy when handing my ticket to the kid who had replaced me.

Dad lost that job sometime in the spring of 1944, as I was wrapping up my sixth year of school, shortly before the invasion of Normandy on June sixth, D-Day. Jobless for some days, Dad retreated to what he knew and landed work with a home-insulating crew working the area, traveling from town to town. Freshly chastened, he returned home faithfully on weekends, at least for a time. Soon he was in charge of the truck the crew traveled in. He drove the truck home on Friday or Saturday and parked it on the grassy patch north of our house. Perhaps because of the lumps he had taken from the Larsons, he began to gulp more whiskey on weekends and stumble home late, glassy-eyed and incoherent. One Saturday near midnight, an acquaintance stopped by to report he was careening out of control on Main Street. I dressed and went to find him, making my way past the movie theater to the pool hall where the proprietor and a collection of his patrons stood on the steps looking up the street.

"He's going to hurt himself," one said.

"Or someone else, the damned fool."

I saw him then, on the sidewalk by the bank corner, swaying on rubbery legs that carried him a few steps into the street and then back onto the sidewalk. His arms were outstretched and low, as if he was about to throw a haymaker. I could hear him babbling. I hurried past the men on the steps, self-conscious and embarrassed. They fell silent as the drunk's son passed by. When I reached Dad, I discovered no one else nearby; his agitated gibberish had been directed at phantoms.

"Let's go home, Dad."

"I'll get him."

"There's no one here, Dad."

Wanting to get him home without passing the pool hall crowd, I managed to get him across the street and headed in the right direction. It would have been easier to deal with a mule. He fidgeted and wandered this way and that, angling to go everywhere but home, grabbing my hand and dragging me with him. What should have taken only a few minutes took five times longer. Mom tried to calm him when I finally brought him in, though she was understandably angry and agitated herself. I undressed and crawled into bed.

"George, give me those keys." I heard scuffling. "Come back here."

Our back door opened, and I knew Dad was headed for the truck. I suppose I should have tried to stop him, but I had nothing left. Neither did Mother. I heard the truck door open and slam shut no more than five feet from my bedroom window. I heard fumbling in the cab, feet searching for the pedals. The starter whirred and turned the engine, which coughed, caught, and sputtered. In his uncoordinated condition Dad would likely crash the truck into something, maybe even kill someone, possibly himself.

Please, Lord, don't let it start. I had put my hands together, folded them. A pedal squeaked, squeaked again and again. He was pumping the accelerator, had probably pulled out the choke. *Please, Lord.* The engine sneezed, firing on the edge of starting but not quite catching. I prayed it was flooded. Silence. No movement in the cab. I imagined my father sitting befuddled in the truck. He worked the pedals again, the starter whirred, the engine spun. *Please dear God.* The spinning engine gradually changed pitch, lowered to a growl as the battery drained. For a minute, maybe two, I heard nothing. Was he defeated? Or dozing? The starter clicked, clicked again, unable to turn the engine. The truck's door creaked open. My prayer seemed to have been answered.

But it wasn't over. Metal bumped on metal, Dad grunted, the engine turned again. The truck was fitted with a crank, my father a man possessed. He spun the engine, grunting and swearing, until at last he drained his muscles as completely as he had the battery. Defeated, he uttered a single curse.

"Shit!"

Moments later the back door opened, unsteady steps echoed. He mumbled something to Mother, fumbled in the dark, dropped a single shoe. I was too keyed up to sleep, but Dad began softly snoring almost immediately. He slept through most of Sunday and went back on the road on Monday.

Were there no jobs in Onida? Was it necessary for my father to work out of town? Or did he prefer it? Why wasn't he home more often? Curiosity prompted me to ask Mother how she and Dad had met, what had prompted them to marry.

"It wasn't love at first sight," she said. "Grandma wanted me to marry him." It was a stunning admission. I wanted to learn more but Mother's guarded manner restrained me.

Friction between my parents was inevitable, given Dad's alcoholism and gambling. Who likes to live with a drunk? Mother didn't begrudge him his time at the poker table but rather the economic cost. He lost more than he won, very likely because the booze he guzzled while playing clouded his judgement. Were there other flash points? I wish I knew. Whatever the reason, the marriage was rocky. Despite that, I heard little bickering between my parents.

About that time Dad began losing weight for no apparent reason, Mother was supportive, preparing the best meals possible for him, but he continued to lose weight. To build himself up, to gain back lost pounds, he drank milk shakes and ate prodigiously, filling me with envy. He continued to wither. His pants and shirts hung loosely on him. He consulted our local doctor. After a few tests, she diagnosed his problem, diabetes mellitus, and prescribed a diabetic diet and insulin. He began to fill out, to regain his interest in poker.

Poker games in Onida were held in various places, usually in homes. The host supplied beer and sandwiches to sustain the players through the night, many of whom gambled until dawn. Dad held the game at our house a couple of times, once when he and I were home alone. The other members of our family, as I recall, were visiting our maternal grandparents. Dad claimed that hosting a poker game was easy money because the host periodically dragged quarters or dollars out of the pots to reimburse himself for the beer and food, taking enough extra to make a tidy profit, providing of course that he didn't lose his profit and more at the table. On the night Dad and I were alone in the house he borrowed two tables and extra chairs from somewhere and set up three tables in our dining room and one in the kitchen, preparing for the night's action.

The four tables quickly filled with players, stacks of cash before each one. The overflow, men with no place to sit, encircled the tables to read the players' cards and wait for a chair to empty. I was astonished to see the pots grow to a hundred dollars or more. This was 1944. The economy wasn't exactly booming in Dakota, and a hundred dollars was equivalent to about a thousand now. Onida's poker players weren't pikers.

Cigarette smoke clogged the air, beery voices grew louder. One man belted down boilermakers and bellowed over each lost pot. He sat next to our coal-burning heater which was unlit, it being summer. I'd seen this fellow before, once when he was drunk in the pool hall some months earlier. Barely able to stand, he'd gotten into an argument with a smart aleck who needled him. The argument grew hot and led to a trip out into the alley to settle it man to man. My buddies and I, who had been watching a pool game, followed them out, as did everyone else. The sober guy pranced around like a cocky rooster, ready to lay it on the hapless drunk. He threw a punch which the sot somehow caught between his chest and his arm. Though his coordination was poor, the drunk managed to wrap both arms around his assailant and lock him in his powerful arms. And just that quickly the prancing rooster became a pitiful chicken.

"Help!" His eyes grew wild with fear. "Help me!"

None of us onlookers moved. This guy had provoked the drunk, had intended to beat him up, and now had discovered he couldn't. Too bad. We lusted for action.

"Please, honey, I didn't mean anything."

"Don't call me those chicken shit names." The drunk released his grip and raised his fists.

"Honey, please."

An uncoordinated punch thudded on a trembling shoulder, triggering a string of "honeys" and more pitiful pleading. The repugnant coward actually got down on his knees. He would not fight. Disappointed by how quickly the event fizzled out, we boys headed back inside. The two combatants followed us in, the wimp leading.

"Get out of the way, you little piss-ant," he said and roughly shoved me aside, an act that turned my disgust to scorching hatred. Had I been a bit heavier, I'd have called the yellowbelly outside myself.

It was the other one, the one who had overpowered the coward while drunk, who drank and bellowed at the poker table in our house. When he lost yet another hand, he stood up fuming and took a wild swing at our stove pipe, knocking it loose and sending sections of pipe and soot flying. Dad, who had been in the kitchen, came in to survey the damage. The man, who was probably in his late twenties, began to curse Dad.

"Get him outside," Dad said. "I'll take care of him."

I wondered if my father knew how tough this guy was, even when drunk. Dad had boxed successfully in the Merchant Marine, but he was now in his early forties, a diabetic, and probably had done his share of drinking that night too. I wasn't sure I wanted to watch.

We onlookers assembled outside in a loose circle. The drunk threw the first punch. Dad ducked and jabbed him with a left before slamming a right haymaker to his head. The drunk grunted but didn't go down; he went on the attack, arms flailing. Dad was too quick for him. He hammered the guy with a flurry of solid punches to his face and chest, and knocked him flat on his back in a couple of minutes. When the fellow wobbled back onto his feet he had no fight left. He staggered home, whipped by a better man.

Our dining room was a mess, the games suspended while Dad and I swept up and washed the soot away. Dad fitted the crumbled stove pipe back in place as best he could. When the betting resumed, I'd seen enough. I closed my bedroom door and tried to sleep through all the noise. Our house smelled like a pool hall for days. We kept the windows open.

Dad soon reverted to his old ways, extending his absences, not showing up on weekends, not writing, not sending money. Our trickle of money dried up. Our food ran low. Hunger returned, but our situation never became as desperate as it had been in Aberdeen, for reasons I'll come to shortly.

After a few days of meager rations, I took my .22 rifle and followed the railroad tracks south from town, hoping to bag a cottontail for a more substantial supper. My friend, Robert, tagged along. My rifle was tiny, a single-shot designed to shoot only .22 shorts. I'd bought it at a farm auction a couple of summers earlier while visiting my maternal grandparents' farm, paying more for it than I should have, $1.90 to be exact. I'd been tricked by a clever auctioneer into bidding against myself. In my determination to claim the rifle I had missed the knowing smirks of those around me until someone asked me who I was bidding against. No one, it turned out. But the dollar-ninety was well spent. I loved that little rifle, its soft pop when I fired it, its accuracy. It later disappeared from my life without a trace. I have no idea what became of it.

Robert and I had gone no more than half a mile when we spotted a small flock of pheasants sneaking with lowered heads from the left side of the railroad track into an adjoining field. South Dakota was overflowing with pheasants. Huge flocks were everywhere. Though pheasant season was closed, I was tempted. I much preferred the taste of pheasant to rabbit. The surrounding land was empty, no farms were near. Gunning for one would be risky but worth a try.

I cocked the hammer of my little rifle and headed to where the pheasants had disappeared, setting off an explosion of wings. Some fifteen pheasants lifted and flew to the south along the edge of the field. I picked out a hen, set her on my front sight, and pulled the trigger. To my astonishment she dropped like a stone. I'd shot plenty of pheasants by then with my 410 shotgun, but never out of season, and never with a rifle, both of which were strictly prohibited by law.

The pheasant was dead when I reached her. The lifeless bird, blood oozing from her beak, represented a crime. Mine. I considered leaving her in the field.

"Going to keep her?" Robert asked. "She'll taste good."

I picked her up.

"Want to get one for me?"

"Sure. If you'll carry this one." I doubted that I could hit another one but why not try? I'd already broken the law. What would a second offense matter? I reloaded my rifle, slipping in a tiny bullet.

The field from which we'd flushed the pheasants ended in a low weedy area dotted with sunflowers. I waded into a thick clump of the tall flowers. Whoosh. Another chorus of wings. I tracked a sailing hen and killed her in midair. Two shots, two birds. Were those shots pure luck? Very likely. But I was a good marksman with my little rifle, and each one was cleanly hit.

To shield the birds from sight, we tucked them under our shirts and headed for town. We edged into town with our bellies protruding. With my belly puffed oddly out of shape, and lugging my little rifle, I imagined suspicious eyes in every window, a game warden in every passing car. I worried every step of the way. But we managed to get our pheasants home unchallenged. Mother was thrilled. After I cleaned our bird, Mother performed her magic and produced a splendid dish of fried pheasant served with boiled potatoes and gravy. We picked the bones clean.

I hunted other animals, not for meat but for needed cash. I became a skunk hunter. An acquaintance of mine knew a surefire way to get them. Skunks have a fondness for setting up housekeeping in culverts sunk beneath country roads, especially culverts partially filled with dirt. We walked along country roads and checked every culvert, flopping down to squint through them, to see if light from the other end was interrupted by furry shadows. Most culverts gave off a mild odor of skunk, but that often was a false sign, indicating merely that a skunk had passed through. When we found skunks, we brought them out.

Our method was simplicity itself. We carried two bamboo fishing poles, each long enough to reach at least halfway through a culvert, and each tipped at one end with a loop of barbed wire. Stationing ourselves at opposite sides of a "hot" culvert, we would insert the barbed end of our poles from each end. When we bumped against a moving object, we twisted the pole, snagged the skunk's long-haired tail in the barbed wire, and dragged the striped fellow out. When he emerged we shot him between the eyes with my .22 rifle. Money in the pocket.

Roughing up the skunks colored the air a bit, but we didn't flinch during the process. People imagined that we avoided breathing deeply while carrying our skunks into town, but in truth the smell wasn't much of a problem. We, like skunks, adapted to the air around us. A local fur dealer bought all we brought in for what was big money then, three or four dollars per skunk, enough to provide a bit of food for the family, and a few coins for my pocket.

But not every dollar I acquired in Onida was legally gained. I stole some of them. A friend and I were hired to deliver advertising fliers, to slip them under windshield wipers of cars parked along Main Street. It started to rain before we finished, and, in an effort to keep the fliers dry, we started slipping them inside cars that were unlocked. As I flipped a flier onto one front seat, I noticed a greenback crumpled on the floorboard between the brake pedal and accelerator. It was tightly wadded, like a scrap intended for the wastebasket.

"Look at this," I called to my buddy.

"It would mean an extra fifty cents apiece."

Not to mention stealing, I thought to myself. It was in the spring of our final year in Onida, 1945. A time when Dad was away and we were nearly broke, the spring when Mother would soon go in desperation to Ridinger's store and request that we be allowed to buy groceries on credit, something she did successfully shortly after her kidney disease landed her in the hospital. But my situation wasn't desperate. An extra dollar, or rather fifty cents, wouldn't change my life. We hesitated, my friend and I, each tempted by the easy thievery yet indecisive. I took a deep breath and picked it up.

When all the fliers had been distributed, we went to the pool hall to change the dollar and split it. When I unrolled it, my heart leaped, and sank. It was a twenty dollar bill. Here memory becomes unreliable. I remember our nervousness, our second thoughts, our leaving the pool hall and heading to the car in which we had found the money. But I can't recall whether the car was no longer there, or whether other people lingered near it, or what exactly prevented us from returning the money. All I remember clearly is that we went back to the pool hall and fidgeted while the bartender took the twenty dollars to the cash register and returned with two tens. We each pocketed a bill and dashed outside, a crime confessed at last.

Thou shalt not steal. Afterward I made small amends when presented with opportunities, turning back cash the few times cashiers mistakenly gave me too much change, striving for complete honesty.

When I was a third year medical student at the University of Kansas Medical Center, my black doctor's bag disappeared. After a prolonged, futile search, I reported it missing, probably stolen, to my insurance agent, Bill. He sent me a check to cover the loss, something like $170 for the bag, oto-ophthalmoscope, blood pressure cuff, stethoscope, tuning fork, reflex hammer, and other items. A week or so after I'd cashed the check, a fellow student found my bag on one of the wards, its contents intact. I called Bill and told him I'd recovered the bag, that I was sending him a check to refund what he'd paid me and square our account.

"Ken," he said, "no one's ever done this before."

"Then I'll be the first, Bill."

When I later interned at St. Luke's Hospital in Kansas City, my bag disappeared again, stolen this time from the house staff quarters, and never recovered. I duly reported the theft to Bill and learned that as a medical student my bag had been covered by my policy, as an intern it was not, a fitting touch of irony that perhaps atoned at last for my Onida theft.

"No one's ever done this before." Bill's words make a tenuous connection. Memory jumps. That exact phrase had been directed to me earlier, when I was a first-year medical student at the University of Wisconsin, a year I started with great enthusiasm, expecting a year of great intellectual challenge. I envisioned noble professors guiding me through the mysteries of the human body, its responses in health and disease. I raced through the first weeks, gobbling information, excelling. But the experience soon soured. Rather than the mental challenges I had anticipated, my classmates and I were fed tiny facts. To be blunt, we were bombarded with great quantities of trivia, much of it to be memorized in the absence of concepts. Certain instructors showered us with dribs of dross floating in an almost complete intellectual vacuum. Others presented information clearly having relevance to the practice of medicine, and encouraged us to reason our way through problems, but in my view these individuals were sadly outnumbered.

Had I been more sensible, I would have accepted the system, or at least tolerated it, as nearly all my classmates did. They endured the year with only modest fussing, knowing it would quickly pass. But I was an immature twenty-six, rebellious, confused, not yet free of the past reported here, not yet adept at adapting. I was scraping along financially, working ten to twenty hours a week between classes to cover my school expenses and to have enough left over to live on, and accepting my lot. But I was unable to deal with the crushing disappointment of my medical classes. In frustration I began to cut lectures and laboratories. I avoided reading even the few textbooks I had been able to afford to buy. I fumed and fumbled. In the end I managed to stumble through the remainder of the semester with mediocre grades.

The second semester was more of the same. The course that most riled me was neuroanatomy, a fascinating subject taught in ridiculously simplistic fashion. I liked the instructors personally but could not bear their methods. Of our remarkable and complex autonomic nervous system we often were told, "You will understand the autonomic nervous system as soon as you understand that one and one make two." Our instructors might as well have declared that we would understand the secrets of life itself as soon as we understood that two and two make four. The little ditty, one that grated each time I heard it, referred to the observation that all autonomic impulses transmitted from the central nervous system to smooth muscle, heart muscle, and glands are transferred by networks of two neurons in series, but this is a kindergarten fact, unworthy of more than fleeting mention and offering no appreciable insight into this remarkable system.

None of these aggravations, of course, impeded me from learning what I considered to be necessary and important, but I ignored the obvious and threw all blame on my instructors, taking perverse pride in cloaking myself in righteousness.

The final examination in the neuroanatomy course consisted of questions drawn from a file of old exams. We students knew that. My close friend, John Sarbacker, dug up a copy of the files passed down by students from year to year. By scanning through the old files and identifying the correct answers a student was assured of gliding effortlessly through the final exam. To me it was but another sign of the course's decadence. I didn't look at the files. On the night before the final test, at the peak of my rebellion, I immersed myself in poetry until well past midnight and slept fitfully until morning. When the final examinations were handed out, I wrote my name on the top of the first page and handed it to one of the professors proctoring the examination. He understood at once.

"Goetz," he said. "No one's ever done this before."

"Then I'll be the first, Dr. Geist."

I knew I was sentencing myself to an F in neuroanatomy and thereby earning a one-way ticket out of medical school, not the brightest career move. The rest of the story, with surprising turns of its own, doesn't belong here. Suffice it to say that I wasn't expelled, thanks to the remarkable understanding and kindness of the chairman of the Anatomy Department, Dr. Otto Mortensen.

Mother's diseased kidneys had become nearly useless during those days in Onida. She was weak, her joints ached, she suffered headaches and dizziness, she had difficulty breathing, her ankles swelled, but she continued her fierce daily struggle with her house work. Until the very end she did our laundry, washing white items lightly with homemade soap before boiling them on the stove in a big oval tub. She scrubbed colored pieces by hand on a washboard. She rinsed everything and hung it out to dry.

In early April, 1945, totally exhausted, Emma Schafer Goetz was admitted to the Onida hospital, where she remained three weeks. These facts come not from memory but from the record of her admission a few weeks later to the Hoven hospital, on May 7, 1945. When admitted there she was hypertensive, a complication of her kidney disease. From the hospital record I know that she was five feet five inches tall and weighed just under ninety-nine pounds on admission. Her nutrition was described as poor. She was given a transfusion of citrated blood and discharged nine days later, mildly improved.

From her history recorded in the hospital chart, I learned her first symptomatic attack of kidney disease had come some thirteen years earlier, while pregnant with her first child, a boy.

After Mother was released from the Hoven hospital, she went briefly to stay with her parents in Java before returning to Onida. They later brought her, and Betty and Gary, who had been staying with them, back to us. Mother noticed her parents improving situation.

"They spread jam thick on their bread," she told me.

I understood perfectly. At those rare times when we had jam or jelly, we applied it to bread like a thin coat of paint.

Two good things happened after Mother returned. Temporarily revitalized by her rest and the blood transfusion, this was the time that she went to the grocer we'd always traded with in Onida and arranged a charge account so we could sign for our groceries. From then on she bought frugally. We didn't eat fancy, but our days of hunger were over. And Dad, perhaps knowing Mother's deteriorating condition far better than we children, began to spend more time at home.

We joked about her illness, Dad, Mother, and I, a few weeks before she died. The three of us sat in the dining room of our rented house one night in late summer. The new school year crowded near. The dining room was brightly lit by two ceiling bulbs glowing through a translucent plastic cover. We sat on our straight-backed chairs, Dad with his back to the dark living room, Mother near the unlit coal-burning stove. I, with my back to the kitchen, formed the apex of our triangle. The younger kids were sleeping, or maybe only Carol was home. Betty and Gary for a time were taken to stay with our grandparents in Java, who had volunteered to keep the two pre-schoolers and lighten Mother's load.

"When Mom woke me up, she couldn't talk," I said, reviewing what each of us knew so well, trying to put a comic twist on the night that had scared me out of my wits. "She shook me and said, 'Mmmh, mmmmh, mmmh.' She kept pointing to the northwest. When I asked if she wanted me to get Dad, she nodded."

Mother smiled brightly as I told the story, and I, too young to detect pain or fear concealed behind certain bright eyes, smiled back at her. I was thirteen, Mother thirty-seven. I think each of us had wanted to clear the air ever since that horrible night of some weeks earlier, but it had taken time to work up the necessary courage.

"Mom said her tongue felt thick," I said. "That's why she couldn't get her words out." We talked on, recalling details but carefully avoiding any mention of the future.

Dad had been playing poker when Mother woke me, unable to talk. I flew the six or seven blocks to the poker game to alert Dad. While he ran home, I detoured to get the town's only doctor, Dr. Hales, I believe her name was, who hurriedly dressed and accompanied me.

"That poor woman," she said, as we neared our house.

By the next morning Mother could speak normally. She forced herself out of bed and resumed being a housewife, though at a much slower pace. She seemed determined to override her illness, to carry on.

I refused to see what was coming, though the signs were clear. Once, when I was planning to hitchhike to the Pierre swimming pool, thirty miles one way, with a couple of friends, a summer adventure we undertook often, Mother asked me to stay home, saying she feared another attack might strike while I was away. Dad was out of town. Eager for a swim, I pestered her to change her mind. She didn't anger but made it clear that I must not go. While I wandered unhappily through the house, wishing I was cooling off in the Pierre pool, she sat alone on the couch in our living room, so terribly alone. I suppose everyone has moments that cry to be relived, to be changed for the better. For me, perhaps no time is more loaded with regret than that day. Why didn't I go to her, sit beside her, talk with her, console her?

I had a modest number of daily chores to do, nothing difficult or particularly time-consuming, but I tended to put them off for as long as possible. To gain time I liked to slip out our kitchen door, loop around side of our house, and escape along Main Street for a bit of play. During our last few weeks in Onida, I made one of my routine escapes and came around to the front of our house. Mother stood on the porch waiting.

"Caught you, didn't I?" she said.

I've lost the timbre of her voice, no longer can hear it, but now, seeing her standing on the porch and hearing her words, the exact four she uttered, her voice for an instant breaks through before drifting away. Caught in the act, surprised, embarrassed, I told her how sorry I was for attempting to run out on her. She stood quietly, her light brown hair glowing like a halo. She didn't rebuke me. I don't believe I've known anyone having more quiet goodness, more willingness to accept life's harshest difficulties without breaking, or lashing out. Had I been a bit older, a bit more perceptive, I might have asked her the source of her amazing ability to endure. Aunt Ella, her sister, thinks it was her faith in God.

I can recall only one situation that inevitably transformed my passive mother into an eager aggressor: toilet training. Her method, which never varied, must have sprung directly from her own mother's teaching. She began the process by slicing lengthwise through a bar of white soap, removing roughly a third. With a paring knife she rounded and sharpened the piece, fashioning an anal probe, a solidified enema if you will. When she suspected her toddler was about to soil clean diapers, she went into action, wetting her pointed shaft of soap, slipping it in and holding it in place while carrying her youngster to the potty. After an interval of retention, out came the soap, down sat the toddler. If necessary, the sequence was repeated. Her method produced remarkable results in my three younger siblings. Each one in turn quickly learned to head for the potty on their own, thus avoiding Mother's smooth cathartic probe. Though I have no memory of it, I too surely learned the power of Mother's efficient white suppository.

One day late in that summer Mother called me to the closet door in the small bedroom Gary and I shared. She had packed boxes of clothing.

"These are Carol's," she said, "and here are Betty Jane's, and these are Gary's. You'll need to know that when I'm gone."

Her voice was firm. It didn't crack, for my sake, I suppose. She didn't cry. She may have wept when she was alone in her bed at night, but other than the single time in Timber Lake when she opened up to her parents, I never saw her shed a tear of self-pity. When she showed me the carefully-packed boxes of clothing, knowing her time was near, she was putting her affairs in order, depending on me to be a good son and carry on. Dad was out of town for the week; she had no one else to tell. I should have been handled it better, but her message rattled me.

"You'll be okay, Mom. Don't talk like that." I broke off the conversation and thus missed the ideal opportunity to tell her how much I loved her, how desperately I would miss her, to settle that between us.

I started school the next day and got off to a rough start in the eighth grade. I don't recall my teacher's name, but she had taught in the system before and had heard a thing or two about me, unfavorable things that probably were true. From the opening day I was in her sights. I was shot down for every minor infraction. I fought back. Smarted off. I had become a tough kid, a trouble-making brat, exactly the kid my teacher thought I was. And every time I tangled with her, I lost.

The war was over. On September 2, 1945, Japan had surrendered, ending World War II. A day or so later I passed the filling station on Main Street and saw Mrs. Larson pull her Mercury up to one of the pumps. She leaped out and danced a jig, celebrating the end of gasoline rationing.

"Fill'er up," she told the attendant. "Happy days are here again."

Nine days later, in the middle of the night, Mother suffered another attack. She couldn't talk. She convulsed repeatedly. Dad tried to comfort her while I ran to get Dr. Hales. After a hurried examination, she recommended immediate hospitalization in the Hoven hospital, some fifty miles distant. It was dawn before Dad completed arrangements to get Mother to the hospital. I went in to see her after a sleepless night. She lay quietly, no longer convulsing. She recognized me, I think. She opened her eyes as I took her hand, but she did not speak. Maybe her tongue again prevented her from pushing out words. Her hand was cool. Did she wonder, as she lay there, what would become of her children? Her hopes for us couldn't have been high. She hadn't seen many family successes in her life. Her eldest son often was unreliable.

Thinking the worst that morning but feigning optimism, I told her she would be all right. Dad and our next-door neighbor, Mr. Stewart, who had offered his car and his help, carried her to the car and set off for the hospital. Carol and I went to school. Betty and Gary were with our maternal grandparents in Java.

I couldn't concentrate in class. My thoughts churned with worry and anxiety. I hurried home after school, anxious for a report that Mother was better. We had no telephone, but I thought Dad might have called Mrs. Stewart. She had heard nothing. Carol and I stayed with the Stewarts and waited. The sun dropped lower. Still no word. Unable to wait any longer, I went to the only public telephone I knew of, the one in the lobby of Onida's small hotel, and placed a call through the operator. She surely guessed my age from the squawk of my half-deepened voice. I listened in as she reached the Hoven hospital and announced that she had a long-distance call for Emma Goetz.

"Just a moment," the woman in the hospital said. I'll see if she's here. The line buzzed faintly while we waited. Minutes passed.

"She was here," the woman said, coming back at last and lifting my spirits with a bright particle of hope. *Was* here. She was on her way home. "But," the woman added, "she passed away."

I held the receiver pressed tightly to my ear, listening to the faint hum of a line open across the miles, an agitated drone interrupted when the woman in Hoven, unaware I was on the line, clicked off. The operator's soft voice reached out.

"I'm sorry."

Yes. I hung up the phone, dazed and dry-eyed, and walked south the two blocks on Main Street to our yard. Across the street to the south Carol was waiting for me at the Stewart's. I stopped and leaned my head against the rough bark of the huge cottonwood tree on the edge of our lot and had my solitary cry.

After I composed myself, I went to give my message to Carol and the Stewarts. I repeated the phrase as I'd heard it. Mother has passed away. Carol, seven at the time, told me some years later that she was puzzled by my message, not understanding exactly where Mother, having passed away, was. Later, when Dad and Mr. Stewart came back, Dad's eyes were red from weeping. To Carol and me he said, "Mother has gone to live with the angels." Another euphemism, but one that Carol understood.

Our mother's final hours were steeped in agony. The admission note on her record from the Hoven hospital on September 11, 1945, says she was admitted in an unconscious and convulsive state, her pulse rapid and thready, her pupils fixed and dilated. She had suffered multiple convulsions in the car on the way to the hospital. She was placed in a hospital bed. Intravenous fluids could not administered. Her veins had collapsed. She died within two hours of admission. Dad, and Aunt Ella, who had been notified and drove down from her farm to reach the hospital in time, were by her side.

"I don't think she recognized me," Aunt Ella said.

Within forty-eight hours arrangements had been made for us children to live with our Schafer grandparents in Java. I objected, wanting desperately to stay in Onida. But older heads, wiser heads, prevailed. Our grandparents, along with our father, packed our belongings. I was of little help.

CHAPTER 7

I suppose I was near breaking when we four youngsters were packed into our grandparents' Ford and taken to Java. I remember nothing of those dark days before the funeral, nothing but the inconsolable aching.

On the Sunday after her death we buried Mother. Late in the morning the undertaker wheeled her casket on its stand into Grandpa and Grandma's home and stationed it in the living room where he opened the top half of the casket and tilted it back on its hinges to expose Mother in her padded splendor. We four children were given our time to stand clustered before her. She lay silent amid our whispers and sobs. Dad came in and lifted up Betty, several days short of five, for a better view. Then he lifted up Gary, barely three. Carol, seven, could see over the edge of the coffin by standing on her tip toes. I could see everything.

After a brief family service we and the other gathered relatives proceeded to the Lutheran church and settled into the front rows. Mother's coffin rested before the altar, perpendicular to the center aisle. For most of the service I whimpered and raged, my grief colliding with the minister's words. I had expected him to eulogize Mother, to focus on her life, on the noble sacrifices she had made, on her devotion to her family. But the dolt rambled on about "her poor children," and paid little tribute to our poor dead mother. I fumed and wept.

The clusters of florists's flowers surrounding Mother's coffin reminded me of my drowned cousin, Elaine. Fancy florist's flowers, and death.

With the notes of the final hymn dying away, our grandparents led the way past Mother's coffin. Grandma Schafer, shaking with sobs, kissed her daughter farewell on her lips. In my turn I reached in to stroke Mother's cheek. As if carved from stone, it was hard and cold.

Out into the cool September air we went. "This will be her last ride," our driver murmured as we entered our car parked behind the hearse, sending me into another spasm. We followed the hearse on its slow procession to the cemetery on the hill northwest of Java, where Mother's coffin was suspended above the waiting slit of ground. A sheet of fake grass covered the adjacent mound of dirt. After a brief reading, and a final prayer, the coffin was lowered, the mound uncovered. Shovelfuls of dirt clattered on the box below. We turned away and drove back to our new home with our grandparents.

Our transition into their home was surprisingly smooth, given that our grandfather was sixty-eight, our grandmother nearly sixty-one, not the best time of life to begin rearing four kids. It helped, I think, that three high school boys had lived with them during the previous school year. Grandpa and Grandma had provided room and board for them to earn a few extra dollars and had grown accustomed to young voices filtering down from their upstairs bedrooms, to the thump of footsteps on their stairs, to extra places at their table. It helped too that our grandparents set limits immediately and insisted we behave properly. We complied. My sisters and brother were by nature obedient, and I, initially too numb to act up, surprised myself by being reasonably compliant.

I had no inkling of the strain we four made on their purse, for I erroneously believed our grandparents to be wealthy. Their table was spread with abundant food, their neat, two-story frame house, though modest and without an indoor toilet when we arrived, was comfortable. They even owned a car, a 1937 Ford sedan. By my standards that was rich. I didn't know they had given up their life of hardscrabble farming and moved to Java with practically nothing to cushion their "retirement." Drought and the Great Depression had been their adversaries.

"We couldn't save any money in the Thirties," Grandma once told me. "Crops were bad and grain prices were low. There were times when we couldn't even mail a letter to your mother. We didn't have three cents for the stamp."

Despite their limited means, they managed reasonably well in Java, even after we arrived. Grandpa earned a small but steady income from his job as the janitor of the town school. They budgeted carefully, spent cautiously, and grew much of their food in their large vegetable garden. In season we feasted on home-grown radishes, lettuce, peas, green beans, beets, carrots, tomatoes, cucumbers, cabbage, squash, pumpkins, potatoes, and corn. Grandma canned the excess vegetables and filled her cellar with jars of food preserved for winter meals.

Grandpa kept a cow. He and I took turns milking her in her stall, which occupied the left rear quarter of the barn-like building in their back yard. Partitioned off in front of the stall was the garage which housed the Ford. Above the stall and garage ran a generous hayloft. Grandma's chicken coop took up the right half of the building and opened into a large outdoor area fenced with chicken wire, providing her Leghorns and Rhode Island Reds room to roam.

This miniature farm within town provided a ready supply of milk and eggs and spring fryers and hens for stewing. After years of malnourishment, we four scrawny kids could eat our fill. We tore into Grandma's meat and potatoes meals, her doughy German dishes. In winter, our main course often was steaming soup: navy bean flavored with ham, vegetable in beef stock, chicken noodle, or potato in a milk broth, always accompanied by wonderful home-baked bread, perhaps Jello, and dessert. Grandma occasionally prepared stirrum, pronounced schteer-um, a simple dish made by pouring a pancake-type batter into a frying pan and stirring it intermittently until it formed into small golden brown nodules. She made stirrum in spring or early summer because she liked to serve it with a side of leaf lettuce freshly picked from the garden and drenched in her tangy sauce concocted of fresh cream, vinegar, chopped green onions, salt, and pepper. And for snacks we layered Grandma's home-made jams and jellies atop thick slices of her home-baked bread after coating it with home-churned butter. We had ascended into food heaven.

When we four kids moved in, our grandparents had no refrigerator. Except during freezing winter, perishables such as butter, eggs, and milk were placed in a galvanized pail and hung on a rope in Grandpa's cool cistern, about seven feet below ground and just above the water level. I considered it quite modern to go outside, lift the trap door above the cistern, and pull up the pail to take out whatever Grandma needed for her meals.

A few months after we arrived, Grandpa had his cow bred and later helped deliver her calf, a perky Hereford heifer. Grandma organized a drawing to name the calf. She put each of our suggestions into a hat and drew out the winning name: Buttercup, which was Carol's entry.

Betty, left, and Gary, right, outside grandparents' home, winter of 1946

Grandpa intended to marble Buttercup's muscles into prime meat for our table. He fed her corn, watched her grow. Nestled in the small pen Grandpa built near the barn, Buttercup learned to nudge herself against the fence to entice our gentle pats and rubs. When she was fully fatted, a choice yearling ready to be diced into steaks and roasts, Grandpa looked into her large brown eyes and wavered. Never name an animal you intend to eat. Avoiding his yearling's eyes, Grandpa loaded her into his trailer and hauled her to the nearest sales barn to be sold at auction into an uncertain fate. With Buttercup's proceeds he bought an anonymous side of beef.

I developed great respect for my unflappable grandparents. Grandpa, of average height, had the muscles and strength of a sturdy farmer. In the presence of strangers he tended to smile shyly and lower his eyes. Grandma was gregarious, voluble, round-faced with rounded girth. Forever busy, she tensed her chin when she kneaded dough, sewed, ironed, or shelled peas. She wore her long dark hair tied back into a neat bun. When she prepared for bed, she untied the bun and combed out tresses stretching to the middle of her back.

Both were orderly, frugal, disciplined, quick to attack their work, quick to complete it. Grandma saved silver coins, dimes, quarters, and half dollars in a small safe in her closet. She wanted her savings within reach, and to have real value, the value of silver.

Grandpa often took out his hymn book in the evening and sang songs in German, Grandma joining in. Their voices came up to us through the grate that allowed warm air to drift sluggishly into our bedroom from the oil heater in the dining room. Grandpa served as a deacon of the Lutheran church, collecting offerings from the congregation with a velvet pouch attached to a long pole that stretched to the farthest end of each pew. Dressed in his dark Sunday suit, a gold-plated watch fob looped across his vest, he watched attentively as the faithful dropped their tithes and offerings into the pouch as he passed it by their noses. When someone seemed about to allow the pouch to slip by without sweetening it, Grandpa stopped its progress and twitched it in front of the tightwad, giving him a moment to reconsider.

Grandpa Jacob and Grandma Katherine Schafer about the time we moved in with them

Years later, when I was a college student and questioning my own beliefs, I asked Grandma, then a widow, whether she ever questioned her faith, whether she was certain there was a heaven and a hell. An unfamiliar smile creased her face while she considered my question.

"I'm not taking any chances," she said, her tone informing me she would have no more to say about the matter.

On the morning after our mother's funeral, on the beginning of the third week of classes in Java's public school, Carol and I walked the short distance to the school and enrolled, she in the third grade, I in the eighth. I took it in stride. By now I was adept at slipping into a classroom filled with new faces. My new classmates welcomed me warmly. Perhaps they had heard of my situation and knew why I suddenly appeared. The school had no kindergarten, so Betty, too young for the first grade, remained home with Gary in Grandma's care.

Almost immediately came another death. Our paternal grandfather, John Goetz, Sr., the man who had brought his family from southern Russia to South Dakota, succumbed at age seventy-five. I hadn't yet learned how badly he had treated his own family, but I saw him as a powerful figure, and liked him. I liked his wine too, and liked the game he played with me and my cousin, Delbert. When family gathered in his home, always speaking German because my step-grandmother never learned English, Grandpa Goetz treated everyone to a splash of his chokecherry wine. He took up his large pitcher, and a second if the group was large, and headed for his wine barrel in the cellar. From his pitchers he poured water glasses nearly to the rim for each adult, something for their appetite, he always said, and then measured out an ounce or two for us grandchildren. Though it wasn't fine wine, I loved its cheery sweetness, its deep ruby tone, its warmth. Everyone drank quickly, the men taking especially big gulps, hurried, I think, by the appetizing aromas from the kitchen.

After everyone had eaten, Grandpa Goetz invariably called Delbert and me outside for the game, the one I, with my ear untuned for German, called "Bollivar salts." Grandpa had learned it as a boy in Glückstal. He encouraged our uncles to come out on the porch to watch the sport while the women tidied up the kitchen. Grandpa lined us boys up on his driveway and stood three yards behind us, tossing a baseball-sized rubber ball from hand to hand and reciting a rhyme in German. Aunt Rose recalled the words for me.

> Bälle fress' Salz,
> Butter will Schmalz,
> Zucker will Speck,
> Kenny (or Delbert) spring Weg.

A translation of the nonsense rhyme, which reflected his old-fashioned childhood:

> Balls eat salt,
> Butter wants lard,
> Sugar wants fat,
> Kenny (or Delbert) jump away.

The German went straight over our heads, but when Delbert or I heard our name in the last line, we tensed for flight because Grandpa would then switch to English and shout, "Run, Kenny (or Delbert), run." When my name was called, I hightailed it away, determined to outrace the ball whizzing after me. Grandpa Goetz threw hard and straight and eight times out of ten blasted the runner squarely on his butt. The sting of the ball didn't deter us. We kept playing until our bottoms were red and sore and we were too tired to run. Grandpa officially ended the session by fishing coins from his pocket and giving each of us a nickel or dime, once even a quarter, for playing his game.

During his funeral I eyed his coffin in the aisle of the Java Lutheran church and breathed in the heavy scent of flowers, thinking that he and I would play Bollivar salts no more.

It was a time when I could not avoid the dead. Only days after the funeral, I rode with four other boys in an old sedan as it bumped along country roads. On a sudden whim, the driver had struck out in search of a rural burial crypt. Had that been his objective when I climbed into the car, I'd have skipped the trip. Death was a fresh wound. I didn't want to disturb the dead. We pulled into the Wolff farm, the reputed site of the crypt, and spoke with Alton, one of the Wolff boys.

"I'll show you where it is," he said. He squeezed into the car and directed us across a rolling pasture. I spotted an unnatural mound of earth rising above the prairie. Beside it a stairway cut downward into the earth. Fine, we'd seen it. "Let's go," I said.

"Is it locked?" Chris Neumiller asked, climbing out of the car.

"Nope," Alton said. "Want to go down?"

I didn't. But when all five of them crept down and opened the door and shuffled into the vault, I reluctantly followed, driven by my need to conform - and morbid curiosity. In the dim light I could make out a scattering of coffins, some child-sized, all stacked on wooden shelves along two sides of the crypt.

"We shouldn't be down here," I said. "Come on. Let's go."

"Have you looked inside?" Chris asked Alton.

"Sure, the tops open, just like you see at a funeral."

"Come *on*," I said, edging back from the stack of dead. I'd had enough of closed, or open, caskets.

But Chris was insistent. He wedged a stick into the seam of one of the large coffins, and, leaning away from it as though he feared the thing would explode, gave a feeble prod with his stick. Gathering courage, he edged closer to his work and managed to slowly pry up the lid. In the opening I saw a shrunken gray face. At that instant a ghostly "Ah-ooooooooooo" filled the tomb and echoed in the closed space. I saw a wisp of hair move in the coffin. Knowing none of us had uttered that sound, six bodies collided in the doorway, six pairs of legs flew in panic up the stairs.

Frightened out of my wits, my heart thudding, it took some moments in the clear air to realize that someone was giggling uproariously. I turned. Alton's older brother lay collapsed by a vent over the tomb, shaking with gleeful spasms. He had heard us talking at the farm and waited for us to enter the tomb before sneaking over to send his spooky howl through the vent.

I slept fitfully for days afterward, dreaming of shrunken dead faces that howled in their coffins, wisps of hair that waved on dead heads. A remnant of that episode may have shaped the dreams that bubbled up unexpectedly when I was about to enroll in medical school at the University of Wisconsin. By day I was eager to begin my studies, enthusiastic and confident. By night my dreams collapsed into weird fantasies. For several nights running, I dreamed I was standing before my cadaver in the gross anatomy laboratory, ready to make my first incision. As I pressed my blade into the dead flesh, the cadaver, who suddenly resembled my mother, blinked in surprise, squirmed and moaned. A dead arm pushed my scalpel away. Slapped at my hand. I awoke in a sweat.

When the actual day came and I stood before my cadaver in daylight, scalpel in hand, I took a deep breath and - after the moment of hesitation I mentioned earlier - I pressed my sharp steel blade against the jut of the chin and drew it down under the jaw to the middle of the throat, slicing through the mottled skin with ease. I extended the incision over the larynx, formerly the Adam's apple in my parlance, and continued to within a finger's breadth of the suprasternal notch, pleased with the neat vertical slit I'd created along the entire throat. I put down my scalpel and awkwardly began my blunt dissection that gradually exposed the unnaturally gray but marvelously broad and thin platysma, the first muscle we students were to dissect. Having read of its action in *Gray's Anatomy* and eager to compare living function with dead form, I drew my lower lip down and in, tensing my own platysma. As I delicately palpated the straining cords in my throat, I somehow knew that I had exorcised my nocturnal demons. They troubled me no more.

Dad occasionally came to visit us in Java. While there he usually took on a project. Once he insulated our grandparents' home, drilling holes in the siding and blowing in insulation from the truck he drove. Another time, when he arrived shortly after Java had installed a town sewer system, he dug the deep ditch from the house to the sewer line in the street and helped Grandpa lay the pipes. Grandpa set a toilet and bath tub in what had been our "wash room," and our outdoor privy was torn down, its cavity refilled with black dirt.

Dad's labor was, I think, his only contribution to our grandparents. I doubt that he gave a single penny to defray the cost of our keep. Nor, while the four of us lived with them, did our grandparents ever file a claim to collect federal or state monies for assistance. They willingly bore the cost of our care. We were family.

During one of Dad's first visits, as he and I talked alone upstairs, he described his life with diabetes and insulin injections, talked about his difficulty living with the disease. "I'm not even supposed to put syrup on my pancakes."

"You could put an egg on them," I retorted.

"It's just not the same," he said, his eyes dropping.

Suddenly I understood. He was fishing for sympathy. Sympathy! Did he think I'd forgotten the times he had left us to starve? Could he imagine the days when I would have practically swooned if a plain pancake, no syrup, had been set before me?

To hell with him and his diabetes. I stomped downstairs, seething.

He stayed with us a week or two and set off, promising to return when he could. I don't recall receiving a single letter from him, ever. Nor do I remember cards, or a telephone call, on any of our birthdays, though admittedly telephoning then was rare among people we knew.

Late in the autumn after we landed in Java, I discovered Grandpa's collection of spring-loaded animal traps, some of a size suitable for skunks, stored in his tool shed. With an allowance of fifty cents a week, not bad coming from frugal grandparents, but far less than I wanted to spend, I saw a way to increase my cash flow. Grandpa gave me the green light to use his traps in quest of skunks, a method I considered more sophisticated than the barbed-wire tipped bamboo poles I'd used in Onida.

I read up on the essentials of trapping, talked with a few local trappers, and got to it, crawling out of bed before dawn to throw on old clothes and hike into the country. I set my traps at the entrance of likely burrows, covered each one lightly with leaves or grass and sprinkled it with dirt, drove the anchoring peg of the trap's chain deep into the ground. Every morning I made my rounds. Within ten days I had trapped three skunks, killed each one with a .22 slug between the eyes. I hauled my bounty home, showered off the lingering essence of skunk that was part of the transaction, downed breakfast, and rushed to school.

I ran into trouble late in my second week of trapping. My little rifle was chambered for only .22 short cartridges, but on that morning I had run out of .22 shorts. I grabbed a few of Grandpa's long-rifle cartridges, thinking they might work. Once out in the country, I worried. Would the longer cartridges mess up my little rifle? There was one way to find out. I put a bullet into the chamber, rammed it in with some force, flipped up the metal piece containing the firing pin, and cocked the hammer. Holding the tiny rifle away from me like a pistol, just in case the thing exploded backward, I pointed the barrel at a spot of ground a few yards away and pulled the trigger. Wham. It worked fine. But when I tried to extract the spent shell, I couldn't. Having expanded when fired, it was lodged tightly in the chamber, rendering the rifle useless. I continued on my rounds.

One of my traps was wedged deep into a burrow. I pulled on the chain. Something pulled back. I pulled harder and drew out the leading edge of the trap, then a dark long nose, a little pair of fierce black eyes, a vee of white on a disturbed black forehead. I released the chain. The skunk scrambled back into its burrow.

I didn't want to leave the skunk in the trap until afternoon. I needed to kill it now. But how? A clump of scrubby trees grew a quarter-mile away. I hurried over, chose the best of the small branches and hacked it off with my pocket knife, feeling increasingly nervous. I worried about challenging the skunk and his powerful weapon with my puny club. The best tactic, I decided, would be to pull the skunk out far enough to expose its skull to a lusty clout but not so far that it could lift its tail. Returning to the burrow, I braced myself and tugged on the chain. When the beast's head and front shoulders emerged, I took a mighty swing, dazing the skunk. But it recovered quickly and scrambled backward into its hole.

Again I pulled on the chain and brought out the head of my quarry and struck with all my strength. The skunk collapsed. I dragged it out and lifted my club for the kill. The skunk was quicker. It revived in an instant, threw up its tail, and fired. The air, which had been mildly mephitic, exploded with the stink of skunk, and a thick wet stream zipped across my shirt.

As I brought my club down, the skunk fired a second volley, spraying my head and face, searing my eyes. My nostrils burned from the stench. Even worse, I couldn't see. The skunk's overpowering concoction stung my eyes worse than caustic soap. I struck blindly, again and again. The skunk shot back. We fought on until the only things I heard were the thump of my branch and my labored breathing. When I managed to reopen my eyes, the skunk lay dead at my feet. Winded, frazzled, sweating, trembling, and spiced beyond belief, I took up my traitorous rifle, grabbed the limp skunk, and headed back to town.

Grandma somehow had detected my return before I dropped the skunk beside the tool shed. When I went inside, she stopped me in the back entry.

"Throw your clothes in the washtub and get into the bathtub. I've drawn the water for you."

While I soaped and shampooed, she took the washtub outside and filled it with cistern water and Oxydol. After soaking the old clothes, she decided to throw them away. I drained the bathtub and refilled it. I soaped and shampooed repeatedly before stepping from the tub. Grandma's nose wasn't satisfied. She ordered further cleansing. I lathered again, toweled myself dry, and soaked my hair with tonic. Having no time to eat but imagining I'd been decently deodorized, I dressed and dashed off to school, realizing that the few dollars I'd get for the skunk was a poor return for my morning.

My classmates greeted me oddly. "Where have you been?" one asked. "Phew," another said. I passed it off. They had remarkably sensitive noses. Our teacher, Mrs. Moser, fidgeted at her desk as I took my seat. Moments later our door opened a crack. The eyes and nose of Superintendent Spiry appeared. He sniffed but didn't step in.

"Kenny," he said through the crack, not explaining how he had selected me out of the group, "you'd better go home and bathe."

"I already did."

"Do it again," he said.

Grandma wasn't surprised when I walked in. We ran through every remedy she knew. I rinsed with Grandma's home-made tomato juice, rubbed lemon extract on every inch of me, dipped myself in water steeped with baking soda, shampooed and rinsed my hair with vinegar and then lemon juice.

"It's not as bad as it was," Grandma said, taking another test sniff. It was nearly noon when I returned to school, trailing a fainter odor. I was allowed to stay. Before the day was out, I came to a decision. I would trap no more skunks.

My grandparents's patience, their tolerance amazed me. They didn't fuss, didn't rebuke me the horrendous nuisance of my short-lived skunk trade. They endured the stench. Having inhaled the acrid fumes of countless country skunks, they knew the air eventually would clear. Grandpa himself had trapped and sold skunks when their money was short. They knew raising cash can be difficult. They respected my motives. It's too late to thank them. I salute their memory.

About that time Grandpa offered me a job as his assistant janitor. He needed help. It was a large school for one man to handle, especially a man nearing seventy, who was busy with routine maintenance and endless chores during the day, and in late afternoon swept all class rooms and hallways, emptied wastebaskets, and cleaned the toilets. I assisted him with the after-school work, a good job for me, and recruited one of my friends, Orville, to work along with me. We labored with reasonable consistency to earn our few dollars a week.

Grandma had intended to keep all four of us grandchildren together, but Aunt Ella volunteered to take over the care of Carol and Betty. Grandma resisted, not wanting to break us up. But small things nagged at her, made her feel inadequate as a surrogate mother.

"I can't fix the girls's hair as nice as I'd like to," she confessed to Ella.

In the end these minor frustrations, not the burden of feeding, clothing, and housing all of us, led Grandma to agree to the separation. Carol and Betty were taken to Aberdeen to live with Aunt Ella and Uncle Ted Buechler and their two children, LaVonne and Larry. The girls left us in the summer. By then Carol had completed the fourth grade, Betty the first. They arrived at Aunt Ella's home before the new school year began, in time to help Ella with her home canning. Work was part of the program.

My five years in Java were predominantly calm, pleasant. No gnawing hunger, no unexpected dislocations. School felt good. With fewer than a hundred students in our high school, everyone could participate in extra-curricular activities. I wasn't much of an athlete, rising perhaps to mediocrity on my best days, but I enthusiastically went out for sports, working my way up to become a less-than-stellar starting point guard on the basketball team my senior year.

Our school began playing six-man football during my junior year. I shielded my hundred and forty-five pounds with pads and labored as a second-string end until fate intervened. Our starting quarterback mangled his ankle early in the season. Being the only other player who had memorized all our plays, I inherited the starting quarterback's job by default and, surprisingly, performed well enough to hold on to the job for the rest of the season.

The next year was great fun. We had two crunching runners, Bob Noble at fullback and Bob Pfitzer at halfback, each of whom could have starred for much larger schools. On our first possession, I'd call on our backs to blast their way down the field. When our opponents regrouped and brought in their secondary to stop our ground game, I'd go to a play-action pass that practically guaranteed a score or a long gainer. I wasn't an imposing passer, but it's no great trick to hit wide-open receivers. Our little team did well in our little league, claiming the championship with a record of 6-0, outscoring our opponents 229 to 56. That information comes not from memory but from yellowed articles clipped from the Java Herald. One of our players served as the school's sports reporter and his reports, published without by-line, provided details of our season.

I mention football not to pay homage to our inconsequential season but rather to laud the now-closed Java High School and all schools like it, schools rich with opportunity, schools in which everybody can be somebody.

I even joined the school's debate team. During my junior year our team reached the finals of the regional tournament where DeLoyd Hochstetter and I crossed swords with a team from our state's capital city. DeLoyd and I quibbled and split hairs and brushed away like cobwebs the specious arguments of Pierre's debaters, enabling tiny Java to trounce Goliath Pierre. DeLoyd went on to teach English in Anoka, Minnesota, where one of his students was Garrison Keillor, later of Prairie Home Companion fame. I wasn't surprised to learn that Keillor has claimed DeLoyd as his mentor, has credited him for sparking his creativity.

During my final year of high school I switched my janitorial work to the morning shift. Grandpa was seventy-three and found it increasingly burdensome to fill the stoker of the school's furnace every morning, so I took that on. I set my alarm clock an hour earlier, fumbled my way into coal-darkened jeans, and looped over to the school to shovel half a ton of coal into the hopper of the stoker, usually enough to last until the next morning. Then it was back home to clean up and change clothes before breakfast. I paced my preparations by glancing at the mantel clock in the dining room a time or two (I was a few years away from having a watch of my own), and heading back to school at the last minute. My timing was incredible. At the very instant I crossed the sidewalk in front of the school, the first bell rang, a signal to students to head for their class rooms. I achieved this split-second accuracy day after day. I crossed the sidewalk, the bell rang. My internal clock had developed atomic precision.

Years later, at a school reunion, I spoke with Harold Spiry, the man who had been our superintendent and had rung the bell. I bragged a bit, telling him how well I'd ordered my morning work, how I'd arrived at school morning after morning just as he rang the bell.

"Oh that," he said. "Do you recall that my desk and office windows looked out over the front of the building? I saw you coming. When you hit the sidewalk, I rang the bell."

South Dakota was a hunter's paradise, especially for pheasant and duck hunters. Grandpa and I hunted every season, primarily pheasants. We never came home empty-handed. After we cleaned our pheasants, we cleaned our shotguns, ramming rags soaked in Hoppe's No. 9 powder solvent through our barrels until their bores gleamed like burnished silver.

It was after one of our Saturday hunts that Grandpa astonished me by calling me lucky. Though he was armed with seven decades of wisdom, I thought he had lost his senses on that day. How could he make a claim that seemed so outlandish? Didn't he understand how I had suffered? I intended to ask him about it, to challenge him to defend his statement, but the right moment never came. Before long I went away to college for a year, then entered the Air Force and was assigned to Germany. On January 3, 1953, unable to leave his bed because of esophageal cancer, Grandpa celebrated his 76th birthday. At his request he was propped up with pillows when his birthday cake, ablaze with 76 candles, was presented to him. With fierce determination he blew the candles out, every single one. Before the month was out he was dead.

When I learned of his death, too late to return for his funeral, I thought again of his strange comment. How could he have been so foolish to consider me lucky? That smug interpretation of my grandfather's statement lasted until the day I completed requirements for my Ph.D. degree in Madison, a day of achievement my parents, or my grandparents for that matter, could never have imagined. On that day I took time to review the odd turns my life had taken. And I finally came to understand, I believe, what my grandfather had meant on that distant afternoon when we had cleaned our pheasants together.

Grandpa Schafer wasn't talking about Lady Luck, the damsel who supposedly dispenses personal happiness, or personal grief. He considered joy and sorrow to be universal, part of everyone's life. What he was referring to was something quite different, something I possessed and he had lacked: opportunity. He had been reared with endless work as his only option. He had no opportunity for more than the barest elementary schooling, no opportunity for a serious education, no opportunity to indulge himself in team sports, indeed, none of the advantages I clearly had. When he came to this country at age thirteen, the eldest of ten children, he had a single obligation: to work and help his family survive on the untamed and unforgiving prairie. I had been spared such an obligation. I had been charmed in ways that my grandfather, my father, and countless others never had been. Through misfortune they had been deprived of an education they would have treasured. They had been deprived, by time and place, of opportunities I took for granted. I *was* lucky.

I'm reminded of my grandfather's wisdom whenever I hear someone proclaim that success is a matter of will, that the speaker himself manufactured his own success. Yes, I think, you may have talent, you may have the drive to succeed. But without luck you'd be as ordinary as my grandfather, and probably not half as wise.

Grandpa shot a double-barreled 12-gauge, a magnificent L. C. Smith with 32-inch barrels, both full-choke. I thought there was no finer gun anywhere. I had an old single-shot Stevens 410 that served me well enough, but I knew I would be a fearsome hunter with a gun as fine as my grandfather's. I screwed up my courage one day and asked a delicate question.

"Do you think that someday I might have your gun?"

The speed of his answer startled me. "No," he said somewhat defensively, "It's going to Delbert after I'm gone."

His decision grated. I thought it unfair. Delbert already owned a fine shotgun, and his father, Uncle Gerhart, had several more that Delbert might someday own. Wasn't I the grandson living in Grandpa's home, the grandson who hunted most often with him? But I recognized my flaw: my name. Being the son of one of Grandpa's daughters, I had inherited the wrong surname. Delbert, the only son of Grandpa's only son, Gerhart, and favored for his Schafer name, would inherit the L. C. Smith. Surely our grandfather imagined that his prized gun would pass down an unbroken chain of Schafer hunters, each owner lovingly passing the prized relic on to his own son or grandson in remembrance of their distant grandfather. It didn't happen. Delbert sired only daughters and later gave the L. C. Smith to

Larry Buechler, the son of Aunt Ella, Grandpa's younger daughter.

It was in Java that my interest in girls surged. Many local belles caught my attention, and I envied the high school lovers clinging together in their steady relationships, wondered how far they went in their private moments together. All the same, I knew encumbered intimacy wasn't for me. Lean years lay ahead, and I didn't know how I'd scratch out a college education for myself, let alone deal with a significant other. So I simply paired off with someone when the opportunity arose, while cruising in a car, or, when a group of us broke up for the night, walking one home. When I became too enamored with a particular girl, I avoided her in self-defense. I sporadically dated a girl from a nearby town during my last year of high school and first year of college, but unhappily avoided relationships even later, when I was undergraduate at the University of Wisconsin.

That wasn't easy duty. The university was bursting with appealing women, but I, strapped for cash and foolishly too proud to date on the cheap, led a monk's life. The hundred and ten dollars a month I collected from the Korean War version of the GI Bill fell considerably short of my costs for tuition, books, room, and meals. I covered the difference by working part-time jobs. A big social evening was nursing a beer and maybe splurging on a plate of spaghetti or a pizza with the guys who lived in our rooming house on Brooks Street. Even had college loans been common then, I doubt I'd have applied for one. I wanted to make it on my own. There were compensations. For the first time in my life I applied myself to my course work, assimilated information, and enjoyed it. But sadly, like Jimmy Carter, I had lust and a yearning for love in my heart.

165

One Christmas while returning to Aberdeen to spend the holidays with my siblings and other close relatives, I took the train from Madison and struck up a conversation with the attractive, well-dressed girl seated beside me. Debbie, a Wisconsin student traveling home to the Twin Cities, turned out to be a bouncy conversationalist, sweet, and appealing. Seated side by side, our relationship quickly warmed. We kissed while still in Wisconsin, snuggled low in our seats as we crossed into Minnesota. Debbie seemed as taken by me as I by her. When we neared her station, she invited me to meet her waiting family. We stepped off to meet them, a fine family, congenial, well-tailored. We chatted amiably in the minutes we had.

Loneliness gripped me as the train headed west, the seat beside me now sadly empty. While stopping in the Twin Cities on the way back, I scanned the crowd for her, didn't see her. We had talked about seeing each other when we returned to the university. But after considering my situation, I knew it wouldn't work. I couldn't offer anything tangible on a night out. I didn't call her.

Months later, when heading for my part-time work in Agriculture Hall on a lush spring day, I spotted Debbie coming toward me amidst a cluster of girls. The walkways were jammed as they always were in the few minutes between classes. She didn't notice me.

"Debbie," I said enthusiastically, happy to see her. The fire in her eyes caught me by surprise.

"I thought you were going to call me," she said, her words cracking like a whip. Then she and her friends were gone.

Dazed by her response, I sought to understand it. When I didn't follow up and call her, Debbie probably concluded that I'd been trifling with her on the train. Maybe she'd told her friends that she'd met a guy on the train, that he was going to call, that she'd introduce him to them. But he hadn't called. She may have concluded that he hadn't given a damn about her. If so, she was wrong.

Though I unhappily continued to scrape along financially and avoided asking girls out, I rarely refused a direct invitation from a coed. Susie, a banker's daughter from the eastern part of the state, sat near me in one of my chemistry classes. She invited me for a beer after our final exam, maybe because I'd helped her with some chemistry exercises. In a beer joint on State Street she surprised me by ordering a large pitcher of suds. After we'd manfully drained its considerable volume and become mildly numbed, Susie ordered a second pitcher. We talked and swallowed, our conversation skittering and foaming. We changed pace with a bratwurst and managed to knock off the second pitcher before she was due in her dorm. Girls at the university had strict hours then. We stumbled out the back door of the joint and reached Susie's dorm door a few minutes early, where we spent precious seconds happily smooching and bumping. At the last moment I reluctantly released her and watched her tumble through the door. She promised to buy me another round when she returned next semester, but I think she dropped out, or transferred to another school. I didn't see her again.

Becky, I can't remember how we met, invited me to her sorority's spring formal. I declined, explaining that I couldn't afford to rent a tux.

"That's doesn't matter," she said. "Some of the boys wear dark suits rather than tuxedos. It would be okay if you did that."

I didn't own a dark suit either, but I did have a dark sport jacket and a pair of dark pants that didn't match. She said it was important that I go with her, so I agreed, reluctantly.

I managed to borrow a car and drive my date to the dance. When we walked in, my first glance froze me to the floor. Every single male in the huge gathering wore a tux, each a light shade of gray. In my ill-looking dark clothing, I stood out like a cockroach on bone china. What I needed but lacked was the aplomb of a Noel Coward. Wasn't it he who arrived at a party, the only male not wearing a tuxedo, and grandly proclaimed, "Now, now, everyone, please don't be embarrassed."?

I retreated to the men's room where I faced the porcelain, shoulder to shoulder with well-tuxed fraternity boys. One fellow wore an avant-garde tux, similar to the others but with trousers knee-length rather than traditionally long, an appropriately cool outfit for the warm evening. As the trend-setter walked out, the guy to my left said, "Man, it takes guts to wear something like that."

If you think that takes guts, my friend, where would you rate wearing a mismatched dark suit?

Becky and I danced once or twice before I confessed my discomfort, though she surely had sensed it. "Let's go outside," I said.

She took my arm, offering her permission to escape. We meandered through the parking lot where drifting duos in tux and evening gown drew attention to my ill-adapted duds. We slipped into my borrowed car and talked. Becky was a religious girl, a Quaker as I recall. She was pleasantly sincere, and seemingly surprised by the speed with which our lips met. I don't recall going back to the dance. We probably didn't. A few months afterward she sent me a note, having convinced herself I wouldn't call her again, along with a packet of thoughtful information written by her father, a medical faculty member in another university. I knew I was headed for medical school by then, and Becky sent it with that in mind. I never thanked her.

During my time in Java, Dad began to drop in to see us less often. He lived his life, we lived ours. During one of his rare visits, he, sat in the kitchen one evening after supper, talking with Grandma Schafer, Gary and me. Grandma was washing dishes, I drying, Gary helping with the occasional unbreakable piece. He was a first-grader then, I a high school junior. Carol and Betty had moved out nearly two years earlier. I started to banter with Grandma, smarting off, trying to impress Dad with my cleverness. I don't remember what I said, but it amounted to mild teasing. I had barely begun when Grandpa stormed into the kitchen and lit into me, his face flushed and inches from my own.

"Don't you ever talk to your grandmother like that again!" he screamed. "Do your work and shut up." I'd never heard him so caustic, had never seen his expression so furious. His fists were clenched, his arms tensed. Standing there with dish towel in hand, I fully expected a blow, but he vented by spewing his hot anger over me. I had lived with my grandparents for nearly four years, and never had he unleashed such thunderbolts. I naively expected Dad to back me up. Surely he knew I'd meant no disrespect. But my father knew his place better than I, and probably understood what I did not, that my grandfather considered him irresponsible. Knew him as a man who had left his four children in the care of their dead mother's parents, who provided no money for their support, who gallivanted around the Dakotas gambling and drinking, working when it suited him. A man who came to see his children only when he was broke or without work, a convenient time to load up on free food, to sleep in a free bed. And, while he was here, he didn't have the decency to control his son's behavior.

My grandfather's outburst, his wrath so vividly misdirected, was instructive. It didn't prevent me from making similar blunders, but from that time forward I was able to recognize my error when, in a flare of anger, I launched a scorching attack not on my actual provocateur but on an innocent bystander.

Dad left soon after my grandfather's scolding. He timed his departure to coincide with mine as I headed for school. The two of us walked together to the nearby intersection and said goodbye. We may have shaken hands, man to man. We didn't hug. He turned and walked to the north, heading up town to catch the bus to wherever. I stood a moment and watched him walk away, sorry to see him leave. As he shuffled along in his old khaki pants, jacket, and cap, I suddenly realized what a lonely man he had become, how hollow his existence. Once a hard worker, bright, a tough and confident guy, now diminished by alcohol and his drab life, his self-esteem oozing away, he faced a bleak future. Whether he knew it or not, our situations had changed. He now needed his kids more than we needed him. I hadn't yet forgiven him for what he had done to us, but I sensed the process had begun.

I stood rigid as he walked away, locked in place with unnatural pity, until he had covered half a block or more. I wondered if he sensed me watching him, wondered whether he would turn and wave. But I had given my own signals, had frozen him out. He didn't look back.

Realizing I would be late for class if I didn't hustle, I turned toward school, wondering when I would see my father again. I hadn't gotten far, maybe twenty paces, when a powerful urge drew me back to the intersection for another look. From there with an odd yearning I watched him trudge along. His steps were not as fast, his shoulders not as straight, as they once had been. Knowing I had little time to reach school, I turned to go. But once again that powerful force stopped me and forced me back, this time on the run. Dad was nearly to the next intersection. I watched him veer left on the street beyond the Pfitzer home and disappear.

On a Saturday afternoon in August, 1949, when I was seventeen and soon to begin my senior year of high school, some friends and I sat in a booth in what we called the drug store, though it had no pharmacy, playing cribbage. I was learning the game, slowly getting the hang of it, when my cousin, Geraldine Goetz, the daughter of Dad's older brother, John, popped in and stood near the entrance. Spotting me, she announced in a loud voice, "Kenny, your dad was killed in a car accident. Your grandpa is waiting outside in his car."

The other card players looked away, seemingly unnerved, uncertain how to deal with the news. No one spoke. What I remember clearly of that moment is the way my cards flipped outward from my fingers and tumbled downward, as if I had botched a card trick. And in those tumbling cards I saw myself running back to an intersection, watching my father step around a corner and disappear forever.

I went to the car. Grandpa shifted into gear. We drove home without speaking. As we entered the driveway, Dad's familiar voice suddenly roared into my head. *It's not the speed that kills you; it's the sudden stop.*

Grandma had already broken the news to Gary. In Aberdeen, a mortician and his assistant appeared at Aunt Ella's home and informed her they bore bad news. Ella sent Carol and Betty and her own two children, LaVonne and Larry, to the kitchen. The mortician, believing Ella to be Dad's wife because he had the Buechler address in his billfold, told her that her husband, George, had been killed. Carol and Betty, listening in the kitchen, overheard the name, George, and knew.

Dad's coffin wasn't opened when it was taken into the home of his brother, Uncle Fred, for the family service. The funeral director, along with two of my uncles who had identified Dad's body, had recommended a closed service. The car crash in

Montana had been brutal, and Dad, riding in the passenger seat before the era of seat belts and air bags, had been killed instantly according to a report from the scene. The driver, I later learned, lived. Before the funeral I had overheard Uncle John say, "It's George all right. He had that scar behind his left ear where hair wouldn't grow, and I saw that."

A complication developed. My great aunt Tillie, Grandma Schafer's sister, was pestering to see the body. The mortician consulted Dad's brothers. After an exchange of urgent whispers, the mortician, bolstered by family consensus, informed Aunt Tillie that the coffin would remain closed. Not long afterward, Uncle Gerhart joined us four children on Uncle Fred's back porch. Sensitive to our situation, he told us that our father looked very natural, that if we wanted to see him one last time, we would be given the opportunity. He said it kindly, wanting to put us four orphans at ease, to give us the impression that Dad hadn't been bludgeoned beyond recognition. I don't know what he would have done had we requested the viewing. But Carol and I, having heard the earlier conversations, declined the offer. It was, I think, a wise decision. Why brand a father's crumpled face into memory?

When we four children trailed the slow-moving hearse to the church for yet another funeral, an unwanted flood of rancid memories overwhelmed me. Why had our father put us through such indignities? Why had he abandoned us? Why had he poisoned my heart? During the service I sat dry-eyed and raging in the front pew of the church. I wanted to feel grief. I wanted to weep. But I could not. When the minister invited us to bow during his final prayer, my forefingers formed themselves into daggers.

Some small change was found in the pocket of Dad's wash pants after the accident. Someone, I don't recall who, gave me one of the nickels. Not having any mementos from my father, I intended to keep it in memory of him. I stored it in a small box I had made in a high school shop class. After a few years the box, along with its contents, vanished.

I have a gut feeling - no evidence for it other than my own experience - that most fathers consciously or unconsciously strive to provide for their children what they themselves lacked as a child. My dad's father, Grandpa Goetz, was a severe father, "a mean man" according to Aunt Rose. Dad himself, as I've mentioned, was kicked out of his home for defending his mother from his father's violence. But Dad was decidedly gentle with us kids. According to my theory he refused to be mean to his kids, refused to beat them, refused to treat them as he and his siblings had been treated. As a less-than-supportive father he had kicked himself out of our house, though I don't pretend to know why. I'm more confident of my own simple resolutions. I would not allow my children to go hungry. I would never abandon them.

At times certain of my Java friends fantasized how it would be to be someone else, a movie star, a famous athlete, or very rich, a Ford, Rockefeller, or Du Pont. Despite my troubles, I never yearned to be anyone else, not if it meant leaving my skin for another's, or more importantly, leaving my head and settling into another. I would of course have jumped at the chance for certain opportunities or traits others had, greater athletic skills, a quicker brain. But even when I considered someone more talented than I, someone with more admirable traits, I always believed, probably foolishly, that my total package suited me just fine.

I don't pretend that I've always been happy with my lot. The knocks I took, the sorrows and frustration, left a troublesome residue. I learned to shuttle the sour parts off into their little compartments, to seal them off. But I also learned, in time, that keeping the lid on too long would lock my gut in knots. That it was healthier for me to open the ports now and then and throw out the trash. When I have a particularly bad day, or when something repeatedly rankles me, blowing off a little steam does wonders. If I can tee off on an inanimate object, so much the better. I recall a time, I was probably in my thirties, when I took the MMPI, the Minnesota Multiphasic Personality Inventory, as part of a battery of medical tests on a day when I'd been bounced around aggressively, treated impolitely I thought. Annoyed, not wanting to take the test, I found an easy release. I skimmed through the questions and deliberately marked answers that I knew, from my limited training in psychology and psychiatry (not to mention from common sense) would drive my hostility score into the red zone. The little exercise provided a benign yet full release, without a single harsh word being spoken.

One of the colleges in South Dakota, now known as Northern State University but then called Northern State Teachers College, traditionally invited graduating seniors from area high schools to visit its campus in Aberdeen. Students and their teachers were offered a tour of the campus and entertained for a day, a marketing tool to introduce them to the school. Seniors from about fifty high schools attended the year my class went, each class nominating a boy and a girl to be candidates for the titles of Duke and Duchess of Northern Day. Our class chose me to compete for Duke, Kathleen Schlepp for Duchess. Résumés of all candidates were sent to the judges who interviewed candidates on the morning of arrival. One committee judged the Duke candidates, another the Duchesses. Realizing I'd probably rate near or below the middle of the bunch, I endured my interview and managed to keep my demeanor suitably earnest. I recall only one specific interchange.

"Nice tie," one of the men said.

"Thank you."

That evening we seniors gathered in the Aberdeen civic theater for an evening of musical entertainment performed by Northern students and for the announcement of the winners of the Duke and Duchess competition. I thought Kathleen had a good chance of winning because contestants were judged on the basis of scholarship, personality, ambition, and high school record. Kathleen was a bright girl, an accomplished pianist, an effervescent cheerleader, a pixie who starred in class plays, sang in the chorus, and competed in declamation contests, poetry readings, and debate. We Java students sat together in one of the middle rows. As the evening neared its end, I lost my optimism, realizing that Kathleen's chances of winning were a stretch. The third place winner for Duchess was announced, then the runner-up. Kathleen wasn't mentioned.

"And our Duchess this year is Kathleen Schlepp of Java."

She'd done it. I hugged her before she made her way up to the stage. The third-place and runner-up Duke contestants were announced and then the winner. Thrilled that my classmate had won the honor I knew she deserved, I paid no attention to this part of the proceedings.

"Get up there," someone said.

"What?"

"You're the Duke."

Now I knew I was distracted by my excitement over Kathleen's selection, but I also knew I had no chance of winning the title; I'd never even considered it. More to the point, I hadn't heard my name called. What I didn't know was that the emcee had mispronounced my name, calling me gates or goats instead of getz. When the news finally sank in, I made my way to the stage in a daze. Thinking it all a colossal mistake, I mounted the steps and faced the audience. The Duke's medal, dangling on a chain, was looped around my neck while flashbulbs popped. One of the photographs made the *Aberdeen American-News*. People said we were a handsome couple.

For being chosen Duke I was given a pair of cuff links by the college, which I've kept through the years, and a tuition scholarship to Northern for a single quarter of one academic year. Financially, it was a trivial award, having a monetary value of less than fifty dollars at the time. But I, realizing I might use it, considered it nothing to sneeze at.

CHAPTER 8

In the spring of 1950, freshly graduated from high school, woefully naive but imagining myself to be as worldly and as invincible as an eighteen-year-old can possibly be, I took a quick look ahead. I intended to enroll in college in the fall, but I knew not where. In that unknown college I would sign up for a "general" course, whatever that was, and follow it with law school. I had done well in debate. Lawyers argued, didn't they? I could do that. So much for career planning. That was the easy part.

What I needed was the wherewithal. Though I was years removed from my more desperate skirmishes with poverty, my pockets were nearly empty. I had managed to put away less than a hundred dollars for college. I needed a job. Aberdeen, the nearest city of any size, seemed a good bet for summer work. Aunt Ella agreed and kindly offered to put me up in her home until I could afford a bed of my own. I stuffed a cardboard suitcase with clothing, caught a ride to Aberdeen, and moved in with Aunt Ella's family, which consisted of her husband, Ted Buechler, their children, LaVonne and Larry, and, of course, my sisters, Carol and Betty. Everyone made me feel welcome as the seventh member of the household even though my presence stressed the already tight sleeping arrangements and intensified competition for the home's single bathroom.

After settling in, I scanned the local want ads and picked up the telephone. By exaggerating my experience with a brush, I landed a job on my first call, sight unseen, as an apprentice to an elderly painter. My new boss, whose name I've forgotten, picked me up the very next day at first light and dropped me off as day faded. Six days a week we labored in a school building in the neighboring town of Bath, my elderly employer teaching me to paint like a journeyman, to prepare surfaces by scraping and sanding and dusting, to load my brush and sweep it in long strokes, to paint sash (the school was riddled with windows). He paid me ninety cents an hour, not too bad for an apprentice in Aberdeen at the time. I rushed along with my brush, painting myself out of a job but wanting to give full measure. Within thirty days, the school gleamed. The painter, lacking other work, cut me loose.

Another ad caught my eye on the day my job ran out, this one seeking an experienced painter. I wore my spattered white painter's overalls to the interview. The genial contractor, E. C. Montgomery, quizzed me about my experience, then put me to the test. Primed sash were stacked in one corner of the room.

"Paint one of those," he said.

I moved methodically as I had been trained. I sanded the sash, poured a measure of paint into a pail, loaded an angled brush with paint, slapped it smartly against the inner pail (no skimming off paint on the pail's lip the way inexperienced painters do), and spread white paint smoothly on sash. I would have much preferred to paint a wall, for I had learned to speed quickly over large flat surfaces. Painting sash is slow work. But Mr. Montgomery knew that better than I. He hired me before I had finished the first window, offering a dollar ten an hour, substantially less than he paid his eight other painters, all union members, but a fine wage for me. I painted sash the rest of the day.

After I had demonstrated my diligence for a week or more, I asked Mr. Montgomery whether I might continue to work part-time during the coming school year. He thought it a fine idea - and thus determined my immediate future. With a trickle of income assured throughout the coming year, I decided to stay in Aberdeen for college. I would use the minuscule scholarship Northern had given me.

At first I pedaled my way to work on Carol's bicycle, which she graciously offered. But my job sites often shifted, sometimes at midday, and it was slow getting around town on two wheels. Assured of a steady income, I scouted around for a cheap car. After wheeling a black 1928 Chevrolet sedan around the block, I bought it without dickering for the asking price, twenty-five dollars cash.

"She runs like a top," the seller told me.

And indeed she did, that first car of mine. She started without fail and rolled along smoothly on serviceable rubber, her vacuum tank feeding gasoline to her four cylinders. Her solid black hulk struck me as too conservative for my exuberant self. With my new painting skills I brightened her up to match my mood, converting her dark, solid-metal wheels to four vibrant yellow discs and enameling a matching stripe, an emphatic yellow band three inches wide, around her sides and back. While happily piloting my one-of-a-kind flivver through the streets of Aberdeen, I imagined onlookers admiring my splendiferous taste. Dollar for dollar, my 1928 Chevy gave me more pleasure than any car I've owned.

Having achieved modest solvency with my forty-four dollars a week and the occasional extra pay for overtime, I rented an inexpensive room with a separate entrance in a private home for the rest of the summer. I was on my own at last, eating in cheap restaurants but slipping over to Aunt Ella's for Sunday dinners of chicken, ham, or roast beef, and for an occasional evening meal during the week.

Once one learns the basics, routine painting becomes automatic. Sanding, dusting, dipping, and brushing require no more than the slimmest skein of neuronal connections to link eye and hand. The rest of the brain is free to roam. And roam mine did while painting that carefree summer. While brushing away the hours, I thought contentedly of my job, my Chevrolet, my self-sufficiency, each warm day gliding over me like a breeze across flat prairie. On the surface my life was tranquil, without stress. And I intended to keep it that way.

For much of that summer I worked in a development of new homes on the south side of Aberdeen. Carpenters, plumbers, electricians, and other craftsmen worked around my fellow painters and me. When the weather was good, a half dozen or more of us often broke at noon to sit outside with opened lunch boxes and make small talk while downing our sandwiches. I tried to be part of the group but never really succeeded.

"This is a good life," a stocky carpenter said one mild and sunny day. "I like working like this. What about you, son? You like to paint?"

"It's a good summer job," I said.

Eyebrows arched. "You don't like it?"

"It's okay for now, but I'm saving for college." I should have left it at that, but without thinking I added, "I want to work with my head, not my hands."

The atmosphere chilled. Faces smirked.

"You've got a lot to learn, son."

I didn't think so. In my naivete, I imagined college soon would fill my mind as efficiently as a gas pump filled my Chevy's tank. And once my brain had been topped off with the necessary intellectual fuel, I'd stand ready to inherit the still-undefined success awaiting me.

I enrolled at Northern on schedule, declaring my intention to study pre-law, and moved into Lincoln Hall. My assigned dormitory roommate was Roger Wolfe, a tall, curly-haired fellow I'd once seen playing a tuba with the Eureka High School band. As did practically everyone in the dormitory, Roger bought a meal ticket for the Lincoln Hall dining room, which served three meals a day. I passed on the meal ticket. Most of my summer's wages had gone for my room, car, and meals. Grandpa and Grandma Schafer had loaned me a few dollars, but after paying my fees and dormitory charges, I had no money left for the meal ticket.

"Ready to go down and grab a bite?" Roger said when the first few mealtimes rolled around.

"Naw, I'm not hungry." At first I was embarrassed to stay in my room when Roger and everyone else headed down to eat, but soon it became routine. I ate on the cheap, nibbling a bit of fruit in my room, or slipping out in my Chevrolet for a low-cost burger. Money dribbled in from the start, because I immediately began painting part-time, usually working twenty or more hours a week. I earned enough to get by.

Beyond his affable good humor, Roger provided a link to a girl I had met earlier and thought was pretty neat. Darleen, an attractive and slim brunette was a senior in Eureka High, as was

Roger's girlfriend. Roger arranged double dates on some weekends, I tagging along to Eureka when he drove up, or the girls coming to Aberdeen to visit us. I came to think of Darleen as my girlfriend.

It should have been a happy time, or at least a time of reasonable contentment. I was living the college life, marginally to be sure, but I had a compatible girlfriend, a jalopy, a job. I had been elected president of my freshman class. Compared to my earlier years I was relatively well off. But despite these positives, I was restless, dissatisfied - for reasons I couldn't pin down. I told myself I was envious of those students who weren't pinching pennies, who had meal tickets for the dining room, who had parents to support them, and these things surely were part of it. But there was something deeper bothering me, something that set off a nasty churning in my gut, something I struggled unsuccessfully to identify.

One day I arrived uncharacteristically early for my English class and noticed my restlessness zoom to new heights as I waited for the class to begin. I knew what was about to happen. I had been placed in an advanced English class taught by Professor Kelly. Formal in manner, thorough in his approach, didactic and demanding, my professor seated us alphabetically, drilled us conscientiously. His unflagging goal was to make even the least likely of us literate, to teach us to produce a decent sentence, to recognize the force of words. To this end he routinely selected words from our assigned readings and wrote them on the blackboard before class, craftily shielding the list by pulling down a map of the world fastened above the black board. As our class came to attention each day, he tugged at the map and sent it rolling upward to reveal the chosen words that we were expected to have looked up before class if we didn't already know them.

His routine seldom varied, and he followed it on the day I had arrived unusually early.

"Cheh-hmmm," he said, carefully clearing his throat, "the first word, Goetz." He knew I was coasting, knew I rarely completed assignments, and he was compelled to expose my negligence.

He had taken his words that day from Hardy's *Return of the Native*. After calling my name, he stepped away from the list and locked his eyes morosely on the back wall.

I looked at the word, *vicinal*. Having no recollection of ever encountering the word, I groped for a cognate, hoping to make a reasonable guess.

"I don't know," I said too quickly, flustered and missing one I should have gotten, too eager to have my tormenter throw his glare on another student, as he usually did after embarrassing me. But he stood silently gazing at the back wall, then shifted his eyes back on me.

"Cheh-hmmm. The second word, Goetz." The room was utterly still, brought to stiff attention by this change in routine.

Tumulus. I didn't know the word, angrily told myself I didn't care. Who was I kidding? I was red and squirming. Defeated, I slowly shook my head.

"Cheh-hmmm. Cheh-hmmm. The third word, Goetz."

Damn it, it wasn't fair. Enough was enough. I studied the list. The third word was *reddleman*. I wanted to scream. A MAN WHO COLLECTS REDDLES. But I meekly listened to my shallow breathing, my heart battering my chest. What was I doing here? Why was he picking on me? I glanced at the fourth word, *congruity*. All right! I could handle that one.

"Cheh-hmmm. The first word, Armentrout."

I felt no gush of relief when released from my professor's probing. In fact, I stayed keyed up all day. I had long before soured on my classroom performance, but until Professor Kelly's sustained onslaught so dramatically linked cause to effect, I had failed to connect my shiftless ways with my growing discontent. But even afterward, when I saw precisely what my major problem was, I stubbornly continued to underperform, failing to take the simple step that would have eased my tension. I refused to buckle down and stumbled to the end of the academic year mired in mediocrity.

It was a great relief to exchange my books for full-time engagement with Mr. Montgomery's paint brushes. As I removed my belongings from Lincoln Hall I half-heartedly vowed to return to school recharged with vigor in the fall but suspected that my slide would continue. I returned to painting, and drifted along in my doldrums.

One day in July when Mr. Montgomery came to check on me, I was working solo. I should have finished my assigned task by the time he showed up, but I'd been goofing off. Much remained to be done. My boss zinged me with a mild rebuke and stood silently watching me paint the final wall, his eyes as morose as Professor Kelly's had been. Why was he picking on me? When would things turn around for me? I sulked after he left, resisting the emerging realization that I no longer could blame impartial fate for my predicament. I was in charge now. But I didn't know what to do.

The next morning, after a sleepless night of agonizing, I went to the local Air Force recruiting station and inquired about becoming a pilot. Korea was in flames. Maybe I could do something worthwhile.

"How much schooling have you had?" the recruiter asked while sizing me up.

"I finished my first year at Northern."

"That should work without a problem. Of course you won't be able to get into pilot training until after you've finished basic training."

It seemed reasonable. I needed to get away. Here was my opportunity. I enlisted on the spot, committing myself for four years. It was the beginning of my separation from South Dakota, though I would return after my Air Force duty and paint one more summer for Mr. Montgomery before enrolling in pre-journalism at the University of Wisconsin. And the following summer, after serving as a photographer for the Wisconsin student daily, *The Daily Cardinal*, I applied on impulse for summer work as a photographer for the *Aberdeen American-News*. But the managing editor, E. J. Karrigan, hired me as a local reporter. Thoroughly enjoying the experience, I returned the next summer to fill a temporary vacancy as state editor for the small daily, my last Dakota job.

When the Air Force recruiter gave me the pitch about becoming a pilot, I accepted what he said. But it was a lie. The Air Force at the time required a minimum of two years of college to qualify for officer's training school and pilot's training, something the recruiter surely knew. He probably misled me intentionally to induce me to sign up. I didn't learn the truth until I was deeply immersed in the joys of basic training, basking in 113 degree August heat in Texas. My fellow trainees and I did close-order drill and drank gallons of water. We shot carbines, the barrels heated to blistering temperatures by the sun, and drank gallons of water, sweating, always sweating. Our barracks, lacking air conditioning, absorbed each day's impressive summer heat, retained it, and baked us thoroughly each night. Our meals were generous and balanced, if not always tasty. In eight weeks I gained ten pounds. Basic training was a valuable experience.

Immediately afterward I went to weather observer school in Chanute Air Force Base in Illinois. Upon graduation nearly all of my weather school classmates were shipped to the Pacific. Korea was still hot. But I, as one of the top students, was given the opportunity to choose an assignment in Germany. I jumped at the chance and spent three years there.

After my Air Force years, I enrolled in the University of Wisconsin, intending to study journalism and later the law. My pre-journalism advisor balked when I showed him the schedule I had chosen for my first semester in Madison.

"No journalism student has ever taken physics as an elective," he said, and offered suggestions for easier alternatives. I stuck to my guns and prevailed after explaining that I had graduated from a small high school that hadn't offered physics, that I thought journalists should be broadly educated and have at least minimal exposure to the physical sciences. But I had a second motive. I intended at long last to apply myself and wanted to be challenged by a variety of courses. The Air Force had taught me a thing or two. Physics was a good choice. The course was heavy with pre-med students, and I, despite never having studied either chemistry or physics, performed better than most of them. By the end of the second semester I had decided to shoot for medical school myself.

While writing this account, I discovered what other memoirists surely know. The process of dredging up one's past to set it down unleashes a flurry of dreams. I often awoke dazed by misty impressions that fled before I could examine them. When I did manage to grab a segment of a dream before it evaporated in the drowsy warmth of awakening, it invariably contained particles of the past I was stirring up.

Desirous to share and compare memories with my sisters and brother as I went along, I sent drafts of each successive chapter to them. By the time I reached the final chapter, Carol, Betty, Gary, and I had vowed to go back to South Dakota and retrace our early paths. It was an exciting prospect, and when we actually revisited our old haunts, the experience was as wonderful, and as poignant, as we had imagined. But when our travels to Dakota were still mere anticipation, I dreamed one night we were en route. With the suspension of disbelief that dreams sometime bring, I fantasized that we were to meet our parents who had returned from a long journey and were waiting for us in our old home in Onida.

How eager we were to see them again, to fill in the intervening years. Each of us excitedly thought of what we would say, acutely aware that we would be interacting as adults with our parents for the first precious time. We would talk and listen and proudly show them photographs of the grandchildren they didn't know they had. We would be selective, of course, for we couldn't summarize a lifetime in a few hours.

It was a crazy dream, and before we could reach our parents, warning bells clattered, exposing the sham and bringing me up to the fringe of consciousness. Not wanting to give up the sheer joy my dream had produced (I cannot remember ever being happier) I drifted for a while on the edge of sleep, drowsy but remarkably alert, and held on to my fantasy, doggedly running over what I had planned to say.

"I don't smoke, Dad, thanks to you and Mom. Remember that time you asked me if I smoked? Well..." And I would tell him what had happened afterward, how he had handled the situation just right.

"All of us have plenty to eat, Mom," I would say. "We all turned out pretty well and none of us lack money for food. Why every one of us owns a house you would consider fancy, nothing like the ones we lived in while you were with us. And we have washing machines and driers and even dishwashers, and of course indoor bathrooms."

Half awake, I told Dad how happily I remembered his driving lessons in the Model A pickup and his green Chevy, told Mom that my memory of her went way back to when she bought that frying pan from the peddler in Java, that I had always loved her. And then I revealed what I knew would surprise them, that I had graduated from college, with high honors no less, and gone on to medical school and graduate school and earned both M.D. and Ph.D. degrees, and that I had a satisfying career in medical research.

Completely taken by what now was a daydream, I imagined Carol and Betty and Gary rattling on too, telling where they have gone, what they have done, since they last were with our parents. I stayed with it as long as I could, until unrelenting reality dimmed the images and I could bear it no longer. Then I got up and washed away the tears.

When I was a first-year medical student, a classmate and I once philosophized about the pain resulting from parental deaths. She, with both parents still living, argued that it is easier for a child to lose a parent, harder for an adult, because an adult, being more rational, understands more fully what has been lost. I didn't agree with her then, I don't now. One weakness of her argument, I believe, was her failure to consider the preciousness of each year together, how painful it is to be shortchanged. Which would she prefer, to be forty, or sixty, when her parents died? Or ten? I doubt my classmate fully realized how deeply a child can grieve. Maybe one has to live certain experiences to truly know them.

Kenneth shortly before he entered medical school in 1958

When I made my commitment to the Air Force in Aberdeen, I was given a bus ticket to Sioux Falls, where I was sworn in with five other Dakota recruits. From there we were taken to the airport and given vouchers for a commercial flight to San Antonio, Texas, with our ultimate destination being Lackland Air Force Base.

I boarded, took my window seat, and fiddled with the unfamiliar clasp on my seat belt. As our airplane roared powerfully aloft, I peered out my window to stare at the streets and cars and buildings sweeping beneath me, thrilled by that first sensation of flying. I watched the scene widen into green fields, lush with the familiar shades of wheat and corn and prairie grasses. As I rose higher than I'd ever been before, I gaped at the expanding view, struck by the bold patchwork of my native state.

I imagined the expanding fields stretching far to the northwest, where Gary, age eight, was growing up with Grandma and Grandpa Schafer in Java. Further to the east, in Aberdeen, Carol and Betty, ages thirteen and ten, were making their way through the household of Aunt Ella, Uncle Ted, and their cousins, LaVonne and Larry. I was on my own. They soon would be. I saw each of us maturing and forming families of our own - and earning enough to provide for them. It wasn't much, but I could imagine nothing better.

At nineteen I was too naive to perceive the firm link between past and future. Yet even then it was clear to me that our parents' lives, brief and unhappy as they had been, had marked each of us, that the sum of our experiences had knocked us slightly off course. But we had muddled through our early years, and I had discovered the comfort one derives from screening off unpalatable parts of the past. The times we had struggled through were still too raw in memory to mull over then. Only in middle age would I allow myself to look back and examine those Dakota years, to begin to understand how profoundly they had shaped me. In weaker moments I've pondered whether I might turned out better had my younger years been smoother, whether I might have accomplished more had I not frittered away my formative years. And once, when roiling in a personal storm, I even questioned whether a better start might have sent me gliding more smoothly through life, might have made me more agreeable.

But when I soared with youthful vigor into the sky above Sioux Falls, I would have scoffed at such foolish introspection. I relished that moment, that fresh, uncharted beginning. I would be all right, I told myself, no matter what lay ahead. The pilot banked out of the take-off pattern, surprising me with the plane's sudden roll, and unleashing a shiver of happiness. Inclined by the sudden cant of my seat, and by the indelible imprint of my Dakota years, I glanced down for one final look at the familiar landscape I was leaving behind.

ABOUT THE AUTHOR

Kenneth Goetz and his wife live in the Kansas City area. They have a son and a daughter. Their son and his wife recently presented them with their first granddaughter.

Printed in the United States
4425